CORNELL SCIENTIFIC INQUIRY SERIES
TEACHER EDITION

Decay and Renewal

NATIONAL SCIENCE TEACHERS ASSOCIATION

Decay and Renewal

BY THE ENVIRONMENTAL INQUIRY LEADERSHIP TEAM
NANCY M. TRAUTMANN
MARIANNE E. KRASNY
WILLIAM S. CARLSEN
CHRISTINE M. CUNNINGHAM

WITH TEACHERS
HARRY CANNING (NEWARK VALLEY HIGH SCHOOL)
PATRICIA CARROLL (NEWARK VALLEY HIGH SCHOOL)
MARK JOHNSON (ITHACA HIGH SCHOOL)
ALPA KHANDAR (HILTON HIGH SCHOOL)
ELAINA OLYNCIW (A. PHILIP RANDOLPH HIGH SCHOOL)

AND CORNELL SCIENTISTS
BENNETT KOTTLER
STEPHEN PENNINGROTH
ADAM WELMAN

NATIONAL SCIENCE TEACHERS ASSOCIATION
Arlington, Virginia

NATIONAL SCIENCE TEACHERS ASSOCIATION

Claire Reinburg, Director
J. Andrew Cocke, Associate Editor
Judy Cusick, Associate Editor
Betty Smith, Associate Editor

ART AND DESIGN Linda Olliver, Director
    Cover image ©Russell Illig/Getty Images.
    Illustrations by Jane MacDonald of Sunset Design and Lucy Gagliardo.
PRINTING AND PRODUCTION Catherine Lorrain-Hale, Director
    Nguyet Tran, Assistant Production Manager
    Jack Parker, Desktop Publishing Specialist
PUBLICATIONS OPERATIONS Hank Janowsky, Manager
MARKETING Holly Hemphill, Director
NSTA WEB Tim Weber, Webmaster
PERIODICALS PUBLISHING Shelley Carey, Director
sciLINKS Tyson Brown, Manager
    David Anderson, Web and Development Coordinator

NATIONAL SCIENCE TEACHERS ASSOCIATION
Gerald F. Wheeler, Executive Director
David Beacom, Publisher

Copyright © 2003 by the National Science Teachers Association.
All rights reserved. Printed in the USA by Phoenix Color Corp.

Decay and Renewal
NSTA Stock Number: PB162X3T
ISBN: 0-87355-207-5
05 04 03 4 3 2 1
Printed on recycled paper

Library of Congress has cataloged the Student Edition as follows:
Trautmann, Nancy M.
    Decay and renewal / by Nancy M. Trautmann and the Environmental
Inquiry Leadership Team.— Student ed.
    p. cm. — (Cornell scientific inquiry series)
ISBN 0-87355-212-1
1. Biodegradation—Research. 2. Bioremediation—Research.
I. National Science Teachers Association. Environmental Inquiry Leadership
Team. II. Title. III. Series.
QH530.5.T73 2003
577'.1—dc21   2003001325

Permission is granted in advance for reproduction for purpose of classroom or workshop instruction.
To request permission for other uses, send specific requests to:
NSTA PRESS 1840 Wilson Boulevard, Arlington, Virginia 22201-3000 *www.nsta.org*

NSTA is committed to publishing quality materials that promote the best in inquiry-based science education. However, conditions of actual use may vary and the safety procedures and practices described in this book are intended to serve only as a guide. Additional precautionary measures may be required. NSTA and the author(s) do not warrant or represent that the procedures and practices in this book meet any safety code or standard or federal, state, or local regulations. NSTA and the author(s) disclaim any liability for personal injury or damage to property arising out of or relating to the use of this book including any of the recommendations, instructions, or materials contained therein.

This material is based on the work supported by the National Science Foundation under Grant No. 96-18142. Any opinions, findings, conclusions, or recommendations expressed in this material are those of the authors and do not necessarily reflect the views of the National Science Foundation.

Contents

TEACHER EDITION

ACKNOWLEDGMENTS

Decay and Renewal represents a collaborative effort among scientists, science educators, and high school and middle school teachers. Our search for common ground has been challenging and fun.

Funding was provided by the National Science Foundation (NSF), Instructional Materials Development Program. We thank our NSF program officers David Campbell, George DeBoer, Cheryl Mason, and Trish Morse for their guidance and support over the course of this project. Collaborative funding was provided by the NSF Graduate Teaching Fellows in the K–12 Education Program and by Cornell University.

More than anyone else, the people who made this book possible are the teachers who spent summers at Cornell, working with us to adapt university-level research techniques for use by secondary-level students: Harry Canning, Patricia Carroll, Mark Johnson, Alpa Khandar, and Elaina Olynciw. Bennett Kottler and Stephen Penningroth mentored teachers and assisted in all aspects of their work in the lab. Cornell graduate student Heather Clark helped to adapt the soda lime protocol for use in classrooms. We also are grateful to Cornell scientists Sue Merkel, James Gossett, and Ellen Harrison for reviewing draft manuscripts and helping us to translate technical knowledge into everyday terms.

Teachers Margaret Brazwell, Matt Wasilawski, and Tim Wolcott piloted draft materials, as did the teacher authors cited above. The following Cornell students and NSF graduate teaching fellows gave valuable advice about the manuscript and its use in pilot classrooms: Rainer Assé, Jenn Dearolf, Molly Moffe, Peter Weishampel, and Brooke Ann Zanetell. Joe Bradshaw (Chief Joseph Middle School, Bozeman, Montana) and Elaina Olynciw (A. Philip Randolph High School, New York City) thoroughly reviewed the draft manuscript and provided helpful suggestions for its improvement.

With cheerful humor and a terrific eye for detail, Adam Welman worked tirelessly to check facts, test and edit protocols, draft diagrams, and provide creative ideas and invaluable assistance with the myriad details inherent in the final stages of getting the book to press.

Leanne Avery and Dan Meyer worked with us throughout all phases of the curriculum development and pilot testing. We thank them for the countless ways in which they provided insights, assistance, and support over the course of their Ph.D. programs at Cornell.

We thank NSTA Press for producing this book. It was a pleasure working with director Claire Reinburg, project editors Judy Cusick and Carol Duval, and art director Linda Olliver. And we deeply appreciate Jane MacDonald's creative flair in transforming our rough sketches into finished illustrations of everything from wastewater treatment systems to stream invertebrates. Composting illustrations are reprinted, with permission, from *Composting in the Classroom: Science Inquiry for High School Students,* by N.M. Trautmann and M.E. Krasny. 1998. (Dubuque, IA: Kendall/Hunt. ISBN 0-7872-4433-3).

Finally, heartfelt thanks go to our families for their support, unwavering in spite of compost critters in the kitchen and countless overtime hours dedicated toward moving this book from our desks to yours.

INTRODUCTION

ENVIRONMENTAL INQUIRY

Decay and Renewal is part of the Environmental Inquiry (EI) curriculum series developed at Cornell University to enable high school students to conduct authentic environmental science research. The goals of EI are for students to

1. Develop research skills

2. Use their newly acquired skills to conduct research projects of their own design focusing on topics relevant to their local communities

3. Participate in communities of peer student scientists

4. Enhance their understanding of scientific content and process

Rather than learning science as a static body of facts, EI students experience the research process through which scientific understandings are formed and continually revised. Instead of memorizing a "scientific method," they discover for themselves the multifaceted nature of scientific research. By studying problems relevant to their communities, they discover interconnections between science and society.

MEETING THE STANDARDS

The contemporary movement for science education reform calls for the teaching of science to more closely reflect the way in which science is practiced. According to the National Science Education Standards, the central strategy for teaching science should be to engage students in authentic inquiry or research:

> Students at all grade levels and in every domain of science should have the opportunity to use scientific inquiry and develop the ability to think and act in ways associated with the processes of inquiry, including asking questions, planning and conducting investigations, using appropriate tools and techniques to gather data, thinking critically and logically about the relationships between evidence and explanations, constructing and analyzing alternative explanations, and communicating scientific arguments.[1]

The Science as Inquiry standards[2] call for all students to develop the following abilities:

▶ Identify questions and concepts that guide scientific investigations

▶ Design and conduct scientific investigations

▶ Use technology and mathematics to improve investigations and communications

---

[1] National Research Council (NRC). 1996. *National Science Education Standards*. Washington, DC: National Academy Press, p. 105.

[2] NRC, pp. 175-6.

▶ Formulate and revise scientific explanations and models using logic and evidence

▶ Recognize and analyze alternative explanations and models

▶ Communicate and defend a scientific argument

Using a stepwise approach, EI research helps students gain all of these abilities as they design and carry out investigations, exchange ideas about their results and interpretations with peer student scientists, and make recommendations for future experiments. A progression of worksheets guides students through each step of the inquiry process, providing structure but flexibility in designing and conducting meaningful projects.

Students engaged in *Decay and Renewal* projects also will learn concepts and skills covered in other standards, including Life Science, Physical Science, Science in Personal and Social Perspectives, and several other fields (Table 1).

AUDIENCE

Decay and Renewal can be used as a module in biology, chemistry, environmental science, and general science courses, or as a resource for individual student research projects. The background text and research techniques have been successfully used in courses ranging from eighth grade through advanced placement science, with adaptations in the level of sophistication expected in experimental design and interpretation and presentation of results.

In a growing number of schools, integrated science or environmental science is taught as an introductory or basic level high school science course. *Decay and Renewal* works well in this setting because it does not assume detailed prior knowledge of any of the science disciplines and is based on thought-provoking hands-on activities. Although research experiences commonly are reserved for advanced students, the EI curriculum series is designed to extend these opportunities to all students, including those who have not flourished in more traditional "college preparatory" science courses. EI pilot testing has shown that students who are not accustomed to thinking of themselves as scientists gain motivation and self-esteem when faced with the challenge of carrying out authentic research projects and then reporting their results and exchanging feedback with other students.

For more advanced science classes, *Decay and Renewal* provides opportunities to expand students' understanding of complex concepts related to the interdependency between organisms and the environment and the complex interrelationships among chemical, biological, and physical processes inherent in nutrient cycling and energy flow through ecosystems.

TABLE 1
National Science Education Content Standards Addressed through EI Research

National Science Education Standards (National Research Council, 1996)	Chapters 1 – 3	Protocols 1 – 4: Collecting Invertebrates	Protocols 5 – 7: Culturing Microbes	Protocols 8 – 11: Chemical Effects	Protocol 12: Composting & Landfilling	Protocol 13&14: Bioremediation	Interactive Research	Design Challenge
Unifying Concepts and Processes in Science								
Systems, order, and organization	•	•	•	•	•	•	•	
Evidence, models, and explanation				•	•	•	•	•
Change, constancy, and measurement	•		•	•	•	•	•	
Evolution and equilibrium					•	•	•	
Science as Inquiry								
Abilities necessary to do scientific inquiry		•	•	•	•	•	•	•
Understandings about scientific inquiry		•	•	•	•	•	•	•
Physical Science								
Structure and properties of matter				•		•	•	
Chemical reactions	•			•	•	•	•	•
Conservation of energy and increase in disorder	•						•	
Interactions of energy and matter	•					•	•	
Life Science								
The cell	•		•	•		•	•	•
Biological evolution	•					•	•	
Interdependence of organisms	•	•	•	•	•	•	•	•
Matter, energy, and organization in living systems	•			•	•	•	•	•
Behavior of organisms		•		•	•	•		
Earth and Space Science								
Geochemical cycles	•			•				
Science and Technology								
Understandings about science and technology	•			•	•	•	•	•
Science in Personal and Social Perspectives								
Population growth								•
Natural resources	•			•	•	•	•	•
Environmental quality	•	•	•	•	•	•	•	•
Natural and human-induced hazards	•			•	•	•	•	
Science and technology in local, national, and global challenges	•			•	•	•	•	•
History and Nature of Science								
Science as a human endeavor		•	•	•	•	•	•	•
Nature of scientific knowledge		•	•	•	•	•	•	•
Historical perspectives	•			•	•	•	•	•

WHY BIODEGRADATION?

*D*ecay and Renewal presents inquiry-based approaches to studying biodegradation, the assortment of biological processes that cause organic matter to decay. Biodegradation occurs in nature and in human-engineered systems to prevent or clean up environmental contamination. Why study biodegradation? Because it provides a wealth of opportunities for students to learn basic biological and ecological concepts while engaging in investigations about environmental issues of relevance in their everyday lives.

RELEVANCE

When we throw or flush something away, we don't often stop to think about where it is going and what will become of it. In the big picture, of course, there is no "away." Some substances break down and others don't, and either way leads to environmental consequences. Through investigation of the processes inherent in wastewater treatment, composting, landfilling, and bioremediation of contaminated sites, students learn important science concepts within the context of issues that relate to protection and enhancement of environmental quality.

CONNECTIONS

Although high school science courses commonly cover issues related to water quality, wastewater treatment, solid waste management, and pollution prevention, students do not always recognize the connections between these topics. By exploring the ways in which all of these processes make use of the natural forces of decay and renewal, students will gain a greater conceptual understanding of the science underlying these important issues.

Students who carry out biodegradation experiments also experience the links among scientific disciplines. For example, composting, wastewater treatment, and bioremediation may seem to be primarily biological processes. However, for optimal performance, all of these processes rely heavily on chemical and physical properties. By highlighting the natural links among scientific disciplines, and their inherent connections to applied technologies, biodegradation research and engineering design experiences can help students to gain a more integrated view of science and its applications to issues of concern to society.

OPPORTUNITIES FOR RESEARCH AND ENGINEERING DESIGN

Decay and Renewal is designed to help schools meet the challenge of giving students authentic and meaningful research experiences within the ever-present constraints of time and resources. Biodegradation provides an ideal topic for student research and engineering design projects that focus on issues of genuine societal concern. Study of biodegradation leads to a wide range of questions related to how organic materials break down in nature or in composting, wastewater treatment, or bioremediation systems. Based on questions of their own design, students can use one or more of the protocols in this manual to conduct feasible classroom experiments.

In addition to carrying out research projects, students using *Decay and Renewal* will learn basic concepts of nutrient cycling, energy flow, respiration, and biodegradation. As they conduct their investigations, students will draw on their understanding of scientific concepts from a variety of disciplines. For example, composting research enables students to learn about biological, chemical, and physical processes such as uptake of carbon and nitrogen by microorganisms, diffusion of oxygen through air and water, and effect of moisture on heat production and transfer. Similarly, wastewater treatment involves vital interconnections among biological, chemical, and physical processes working together in the decomposition of organic wastes.

CRITICAL THINKING

"Plants photosynthesize and animals respire." "Plants get their food from the soil." "All bacteria are harmful." These common misconceptions affect student understandings about basic biological and ecological processes such as photosynthesis, respiration, nutrient cycling, and energy flow. Students can tackle their misconceptions by designing experiments that will test their understandings. Do plants produce CO_2, or just use it? What are the critical factors for plant growth? Will composting or wastewater treatment systems function without bacteria?

Sometimes students come up with unexpected results, and their first response is to assume that the data are incorrect, and so they must have done something wrong. However, this may not be the case, and tracking down the source of the discrepant results provides an ideal opportunity for critical thinking and in-depth analysis. Maybe something did go wrong with the experiment, but another possibility is that the initial expectations were incorrect. Classroom discussions and library and Internet research may help to sort this out. If there is time for follow-up experiments, they can be used to test newly generated predictions about the expected outcomes.

Table 2 lists intended learning outcomes for students engaged in EI biodegradation research and technological design.

TABLE 2
Intended Learning Outcomes

Skills: Students will gain the ability to

▶ Conduct scientific research, starting with well-defined protocols and progressing to open-ended research projects

▶ Define a biodegradation research question, then plan and carry out an experiment to address this question

▶ Engage in engineering design, including planning, constructing and testing a device, assessing cost, and then presenting and critiquing the results with fellow students

▶ Work collaboratively to design experiments or engineering designs, interpret results, and critically analyze ideas and conclusions

▶ Analyze data and draw conclusions about the research or design results

▶ Write a concise and accurate summary of methods, results, and conclusions

▶ Engage in peer review to exchange constructive criticism of data analysis, interpretations, and conclusions

▶ Use feedback from fellow students to revise or justify reports and presentations

Concepts: Students will gain the understanding that

▶ Life on Earth depends on cycling of carbon and other nutrients, and on flow of energy from the Sun to producers, consumers, and decomposers

▶ Bacteria and fungi play essential roles in nutrient cycling and energy flow on land and in water

▶ Decomposers play crucial but often hidden roles in food webs and energy pyramids

▶ Through photosynthesis, producers use solar energy, CO_2, and water to create food in the form of chemical energy. Consumers, including decomposers, obtain energy by eating other organisms or their wastes

▶ Through cellular respiration, living things use the chemical energy stored in organic compounds, releasing CO_2, water, and heat as by-products

▶ Humans harness natural forces of decay in order to protect or clean up the environment through composting, wastewater treatment, and bioremediation

▶ Science is multidisciplinary and relevant to societal concerns

▶ Scientists and engineers work both individually and collaboratively, reviewing each other's work to provide feedback on experimental design and interpretation of results

▶ Scientific understandings are tentative, subject to change with new discoveries. Peer review among scientists helps to sort genuine discoveries from incomplete or faulty work

LEVELS OF INQUIRY

Environmental Inquiry (EI) is organized into two levels of inquiry modeled after research activities conducted by professional scientists. Students first learn standard research methods, or protocols. Then they explore possibilities for using these protocols to address relevant research or technological design questions. After planning and carrying out one or more interactive research experiments or engineering designs, students present and discuss the results with their peers and possibly with interested community groups.

EI research represents a continuum, with progressively increasing levels of student responsibility for the design of the investigations. There also is a progression in interaction among students as they learn to critically analyze their results, argue among alternative interpretations, and communicate their findings to fellow student scientists (see Figure 1).

GUIDING PROTOCOL-LEVEL INQUIRY

EI protocols introduce students to standard laboratory and field methods that have been adapted from university research to be feasible and safe for use by high school students. Experience with the protocols helps students to develop basic skills and understandings they will be able to use in designing and carrying out scientific investigations.

Protocols differ from traditional school laboratory exercises because they are research techniques rather than demonstrations, so the teacher does not necessarily know the outcome in advance. The **Data Forms** included in the *Student Edition* will guide students through the appropriate steps in data analysis and interpretation, including the final step of generating ideas for follow-up experiments.

Although at this level the students may not develop their own plan of work, it still is important for them to recognize what the research question is and how this question relates to the work they will be carrying out. The **Protocol Planning Form** (p. 96) should help them to make these connections.

Collaborative work is integral to EI research, including at the protocol level (Table 3). This collaboration includes the process of peer review, through which students exchange feedback about their work. Although peer review is used primarily at the interactive research level, students who have completed a protocol can critique each other's results and conclusions and exchange written feedback using the **Data Analysis Peer Review Form** (p. 97). This step introduces students to the benefits of exchanging constructive criticism, both to sharpen their own thinking and to provide advice to their peers.

FIGURE 1
Levels of Inquiry in EI

NOTE: Many different sequences are possible, depending on student ability levels and interests as well as considerations of time and curriculum.

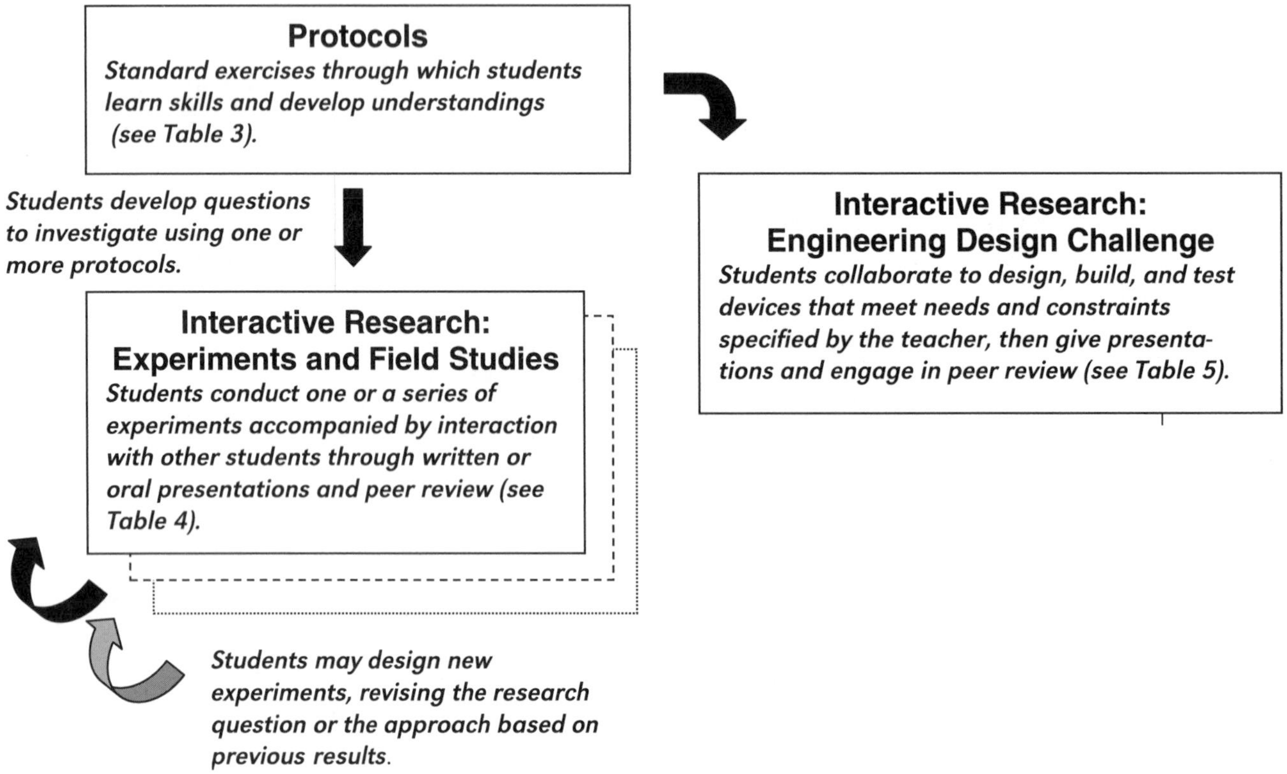

Protocols
Standard exercises through which students learn skills and develop understandings (see Table 3).

Students develop questions to investigate using one or more protocols.

Interactive Research: Engineering Design Challenge
Students collaborate to design, build, and test devices that meet needs and constraints specified by the teacher, then give presentations and engage in peer review (see Table 5).

Interactive Research: Experiments and Field Studies
Students conduct one or a series of experiments accompanied by interaction with other students through written or oral presentations and peer review (see Table 4).

Students may design new experiments, revising the research question or the approach based on previous results.

TABLE 3
Steps in Carrying Out an EI Protocol

Activity	Collaborative and Individual Work	Peer Review Process
Planning to use a protocol	Students work individually or collaboratively to fill out the **Protocol Planning Form** (p. 96).	N.A.
Carrying out a protocol	Students work in groups to conduct a protocol.	N.A.
Analyzing and presenting the results	Students work individually or collaboratively to report and analyze their data, then write individual lab reports.	Before students write their reports, groups pair up to discuss and compare results using the **Data Analysis Peer Review Form** (p. 97).

CONDUCTING INTERACTIVE RESEARCH

Having mastered one or more of the protocols, students use these techniques to carry out open-ended research or technological design projects. This level is called interactive research because it emphasizes collaborative knowledge building and information exchange. Through these collaborative interactions, students not only improve their own work and enhance their critical thinking skills, they also model an essential process underlying all professional scientific communities.

One of the goals of interactive research is to dispel the common misconception among students that science is a career that is pursued in isolation. Students commonly do not realize the extent to which scientists work together to discuss ideas, share findings, give each other feedback, and collaborate on joint projects. Scientists also communicate with larger, non-science communities. Scientific findings inform public decision-making, and, in turn, community priorities help shape scientific research agendas.

Experiments and Field Studies

At the interactive research level, students work in groups to plan and conduct experiments or field studies (Table 4), then communicate their findings and build on each other's experiences as they carry out the following processes:

◗ Narrowing down an interesting research question

◗ Planning an appropriate experiment or series of experiments

◗ Sharing observations and advice with other students who are conducting similar studies

◗ Discussing various possible interpretations of research results

◗ Presenting findings in oral or written form

◗ Participating in peer review of research presentations

◗ Recommending ideas and approaches for future experiments

TABLE 4
Collaboration and Peer Review in Experiments and Field Studies

Activity	Collaborative Work	Peer Review Process
Planning an experiment	Students work together to brainstorm research ideas, then fill out **Choosing a Research Topic** (p. 110) and **Interactive Research Planning Form #1** or **#2** (pp. 113 and 115).	Student groups are paired up to discuss and refine research plans using the **Experimental Design Peer Review Form** (p. 124).
Carrying out the experiment	Students work in groups to conduct experiments.	N.A.
Analyzing and presenting the results	Students collaborate to analyze their data, then write research reports using the **Research Report Form** (p. 120) or create posters using the **Poster Guidelines** (p. 123).	Students present their research results, then exchange feedback using the **Research Report Peer Review Form** (p. 125) or **Poster Peer Review Form** (p. 126). Final reports incorporate changes generated through peer review.

Wastewater Treatment Design Challenge

A second form of interactive research is the design challenge, in which students apply skills in mathematical analysis, scientific inquiry, and technological design toward solving a specified problem within certain constraints. Design challenges differ from experiments in that the teacher specifies a specific problem for the students to address. Working with the provided specifications, students select, build, and test a design they have chosen to be optimal in balancing performance with cost. After demonstrating their devices, student teams assess the performance, cost, and strengths and weaknesses of each. This process is included in interactive research because the students demonstrate their devices publicly and share in the process of peer review (see Table 5).

In *Decay and Renewal,* students are challenged to plan and build devices to treat simulated wastewater. This challenge provides an engaging way for students to apply what they have learned about the science of biodegradation while working to solve a problem of genuine relevance. Student teams define the problem, identify alternative solutions, and select their best design based on consideration of factors including cost, safety, and anticipated effectiveness. After building, testing, and refining their devices, students give presentations and evaluate each other's work using the **Design Challenge Peer Review Form** (p. 140).

TABLE 5
Collaboration and Peer Review in a Design Challenge

Activity	Collaborative Work	Peer Review Process
Designing alternatives and choosing the best alternative	In response to a teacher-specified design problem, students work in groups to brainstorm ideas and then choose the best alternative using the **Design Selection Rubric** (p. 137) and present it to the teacher using the **Design Proposal Form** (p. 138).	N.A.
Building and using a device	Students work in groups to build, test, refine, and then run a wastewater treatment unit.	N.A.
Analyzing and presenting the results	Students collaborate to evaluate the effectiveness of their device and to plan a presentation of their work.	Students demonstrate their device and their assessment of its performance, then exchange feedback using the **Design Challenge Peer Review Form** (p. 140).

GUIDING
STUDENT INQUIRY

ABOUT THE *STUDENT EDITION*

The *Student Edition* is divided into four sections:

Section 1—Understanding Biodegradation

Three chapters of background text cover basic concepts in biodegradation as it occurs in nature and as it is used in the processes of composting, wastewater treatment, and bioremediation.

Section 2—Biodegradation Protocols: Introduction to Research

A series of 14 protocols providing specific instruction on research techniques related to the study of biodegradation.

Section 3—Interactive Research: Experiments and Field Studies

Guidance for developing relevant and interesting research projects using the protocols in Section 2.

Section 4—Interactive Research: Wastewater Treatment Design Challenge

Instructions for conducting an engineering design challenge in which students design and build systems for treating simulated wastewater using physical, biological, and chemical processes.

Sections 2, 3, and 4 include forms designed to guide students through the processes of planning a research or design project, analyzing and presenting their results, and engaging in peer review.

SECTION 1

UNDERSTANDING BIODEGRADATION

MODEL RESPONSES TO DISCUSSION QUESTIONS

Each chapter of the background text in the *Student Edition* (Section 1) concludes with questions that you can use for class discussions or homework essays to help students reflect on the concepts presented. Below you will find model responses to the discussion questions.

Chapter 1: Natural Forces of Decay and Renewal

▶ Could we live without microbes? How do they affect humans and the environment?

No, we couldn't live without microbes. It is a common misconception that humans would be better off without bacteria and fungi, which are thought of as nuisance organisms that cause food to rot and cause some human diseases such as anthrax and bacterial pneumonia. Although bacteria and fungi do play these "nuisance" roles, they also are essential to life on Earth because of the critical role they play in breaking down organic materials and releasing carbon, nitrogen, and other nutrients in forms that can be used to support further life.

▶ Why do we say that nutrients "cycle" but that energy "flows" in ecosystems? What roles do decomposers play in these processes?

Energy is neither created nor destroyed, but we think of it as flowing rather than cycling through ecosystems because life on Earth requires continual input of energy from the Sun. Photosynthetic organisms convert solar energy to chemical energy, which is used by the producers themselves and by all types of consumers and decomposers. Without continued input of solar energy, life as we know it would end because at each level of every food web much of the chemical energy gets lost in the form of heat. Energy flow through an ecosystem is represented as a pyramid because of these losses in chemical energy that is available as food.

Unlike energy, the Earth does not receive new inputs of nutrients such as carbon. Instead, carbon and other nutrients constantly cycle between living and nonliving forms. For example, organisms incorporate carbon into organic compounds such as sugars, carbohydrates, and proteins. The carbon later gets converted back into inorganic form and carbon dioxide gets released back into the environment through respiration by all types of organisms—producers, consumers, and decomposers.

▶ If matter can be neither created nor destroyed, where does it go when plants or animals decompose?

A common misconception among students is that soils get deeper each year as leaves and other organic materials fall and decompose. Up to a certain point, soils do get deeper, but decomposition doesn't stop with formation of the organic component of soil. Instead, decomposition continues in the soil, gradually converting organic compounds into inorganic ones including carbon dioxide and water.

Chapter 2. Harnessing Natural Decay

▶ Biodegradable plastics sometimes are mentioned as a useful way to slow the rate at which landfills are filling up. Would you say that they are a good solution to this problem? Why or why not?

Biodegradable plastics do not degrade well in landfills because the environmental conditions do not support high levels of microbial growth. Plastics generally make up only 10% of landfill volume, so even if they did degrade under landfill conditions, this would not solve landfill capacity problems. However, if biodegradable plastics break down quickly in the sun or rain, they may help to reduce problems caused by litter along roadsides and in waterways. And if they readily break down in compost, they can be used for disposable dishes and utensils that get composted along with food scraps.

▶ What do you think determines how many and what types of microbes will be present in a sample of compost?

The number and types of microorganisms will depend on the food supply—how much and what type of organic matter is available. At the beginning of the composting process, there is a lot of readily degradable organic matter. At the end, all that is left are the compounds that are quite resistant to decay. Different types of microbes are specialized in breaking down different types of compounds, and each thrives when the right mix of ingredients is available. Microbe populations also will change according to physical and chemical factors, including temperature, moisture, pH, and oxygen.

▶ Do you think the microbes in compost are the same or different species from the ones in wastewater? Why?

Microbes are found everywhere—in air, water, food, and human digestive tracts, as well as in soil, compost, and sludge from wastewater treatment operations. Some of these microbes are quite specialized and can be found only under specific environmental conditions. Others are generalists and are adapted to life under a wide range of conditions. So, some of the same microbe species are likely to be found both in compost and in wastewater treatment systems, and others will be found exclusively in one or the other of these environments.

Chapter 3. Bioremediation: Using Microbes to Clean Up Contaminated Sites

▶ What do wastewater treatment, composting, and bioremediation have in common?

These three processes are designed to accelerate natural processes of decay and renewal in order to protect or improve environmental quality. All three depend on microorganisms to break down organic matter or pollutant chemicals by using it as a source of food. In waste-water treatment, microbes break down organic matter in sewage so that it will not over-whelm the natural purification processes in lakes, streams, or other water bodies. In composting, microbes break down organic matter and create a useful soil amendment. And in bioremediation, microbes break down environmental contaminants such as TNT or petroleum products into nontoxic or less toxic forms.

▶ How can microbes get food energy from toxic chemicals such as TNT or motor oil?

Toxicity can be a confusing concept because it depends on the type of organism as well as the type of chemical. There are many compounds that are highly toxic to humans but provide useful food to the right sort of microorganism. In bioremediation, scientists work to find ways to enhance the growth of these microbes so that they will break down contaminants into forms that are not harmful to humans or other organisms in the environment.

▶ Why is bioremediation a useful cleanup strategy at some sites but not others?

Bioremediation provides a technique for cleaning up pollution through natural biodegradation processes. For these natural processes to work, microbes need to be able to use the contaminant as a source of food. Therefore, bioremediation is most suited to sites that are contaminated with compounds such as petroleum products that are hazardous to humans and the environment but are useful food sources to microbes.

BIODEGRADATION PROTOCOLS:

INTRODUCTION TO RESEARCH

The protocols in this manual provide techniques for a wide range of experiments related to biodegradation: finding and identifying decomposer organisms, measuring chemical effects of biodegradation, building miniature systems for composting or landfilling, and culturing microbes that can perform bioremediation.

Protocols 1–4—Looking for Invertebrates. These protocols provide methods for collecting and observing invertebrates that live in soil, compost, or aquatic habitats. The first three protocols apply to soil and compost samples. For large invertebrates such as earthworms, sow bugs, and centipedes, the "pick and sort" method described in Protocol 1 works well. For smaller invertebrates, a Berlese funnel concentrates creatures by collecting them in a beaker (Protocol 2). Tiny invertebrates that live in the films of water surrounding particles of organic matter or soil are best collected using wet extraction, a variation of the Berlese funnel in which the sample is soaked in water (Protocol 3). Collection and observation of aquatic invertebrates is covered in Protocol 4.

Protocols 5–7—Studying Microorganisms. Protocol 5 provides instructions for viewing microscopic decomposer organisms. If you want to isolate bacteria and fungi so that you can observe them separately, Protocols 6 and 7 tell how to grow these microbes in laboratory cultures and then observe them under a microscope.

Protocols 8–11—Chemical Effects of Biodegradation. As decomposers break down organic matter, they use oxygen and produce carbon dioxide. Students therefore can estimate the rate at which biodegradation is taking place by measuring the rate of change of either of these gases, on land or in water.

Protocol 12—Building and Using Bioreactors for Compost and Landfill Experiments. Scientists use bench-scale bioreactors to research biological, chemical, and physical processes in composting systems. Using soda bottles, students can construct inexpensive but highly versatile bioreactors, which they can use for a wide range of biodegradation experiments.

Protocols 13–14—Bioremediation. These protocols provide techniques for finding and culturing microorganisms that can break down motor oil. Once students have mastered these microbiological techniques, they can go on to perform experiments on ways to enhance the growth of selected microbes or to test their effectiveness in degrading oil or other pollutants.

Although the protocols are numbered, you are not likely to use them all or to carry them out in the order presented. Instead, it makes sense to begin by deciding your overall purpose, then choosing suitable protocols to reach this goal. For example, if you want your students to learn about food webs, you could start them out with one or more of the protocols for collecting and sorting invertebrates. If you're more interested in chemical cycles, then the protocols for measuring chemical effects of biodegradation would be a more logical place to start.

PROVIDING STERILE CONDITIONS FOR MICROBIOLOGY EXPERIMENTS

In Protocols 6, 7, 13, and 14, students will be culturing microorganisms. For safety purposes, they should wear goggles and gloves. To provide as sanitary a work area as possible, they should clean the work surface with a disinfectant solution before beginning their work with cultures.

The following procedures will help to prevent contamination of cultures but are optional if you are worried about student safety around Bunsen burner flames. Ideally, you would like to have a Bunsen burner burning at all times when working with sterile flasks or bottles because the flame will create an updraft that helps to prevent contaminants from getting into the flasks. Flaming the mouths of the flasks and the tips of the pipettes helps to burn off contaminants.

If you prefer not to have your students working with flames, instruct them simply to keep their fingers and non-sterile objects out of the openings.

If you do not have access to an autoclave, you can use a pressure cooker for sterilization of solutions and small equipment. Instead of sterilizing pipettes, spreading rods, inoculating loops, and petri dishes, you can purchase sterile disposables.

DISPOSING OF MICROBIAL CULTURES

Caution: All cultures should be sterilized before cleaning or disposal of petri dishes. Sterilize cultures in glass dishes for 20 minutes at 121°C in an autoclave or pressure cooker. To sterilize cultures in disposable dishes, add approximately 12 mL of 10% bleach solution to each plate, allow them to sit for 15 minutes, then pour the liquid down the drain. After sterilization, disposable petri dishes can be discarded with normal trash and reusable ones can be washed for further use.

ADVANCE PREPARATIONS FOR PROTOCOL 5

To make 0.85% NaCl (saline solution), dissolve 8.5 g NaCl in approximately 750 mL distilled water. Dilute to 1 L with distilled water and mix thoroughly.

If you decide to stain the slides to highlight bacteria, you can purchase methylene blue solution (Loeffler's bacterial stain) ready-made or make your own by adding 1.6 g methylene blue chloride to 100 mL 95% ethanol, then mixing 30 mL of this solution with 100 mL of 0.01% aqueous solution of KOH.

ADVANCE PREPARATIONS FOR PROTOCOL 6

See instructions above for preparing saline and methylene blue solutions.

Sterilize the following materials, or provide sterile disposable equivalents where appropriate (quantities are per student group):

▶ 5 test tubes with caps

▶ 1 10-mL pipette

▶ 5 1-mL pipettes

▶ 3 0.1-mL pipettes

▶ 3 bacteriological spreading rods or cotton swabs

In addition, each student group will need:

▶ 90 mL phosphate buffer solution (sterile)

▶ 3 petri dishes containing TSA agar (sterile)

Preparing TSA Agar and Phosphate Buffer Solution

Materials

▶ 2 g trypticase soy agar

▶ 7.5 g bacto agar

▶ 500 mL distilled water in 1 L Erlenmeyer flask with foil cap

▶ 34 g KH_2PO_4

▶ 1000 mL distilled water in 1 L Erlenmeyer flask

▶ a few drops of NaOH or HCl (for pH adjustment)

▶ 1 250-mL Erlenmeyer flask with foil cap for each student group

Procedure

1. Make TSA mixture by mixing 2 g trypticase soy agar, 7.5 g bacto agar, and 500 mL distilled water in a 1 L Erlenmeyer flask. Cover loosely with aluminum foil. (This makes enough to fill 25 petri dishes.)

2. Make phosphate buffer solution by mixing 34 g KH_2PO_4 into 1000 mL distilled water and then adjust the pH to 7. For each student group, measure 90 mL phosphate buffer solution into a 250 mL Erlenmeyer flask and cover with foil.

3. Sterilize the covered flasks containing TSA agar and phosphate buffer solutions for 20 minutes at 121°C in an autoclave or pressure cooker.

4. After the TSA mixture has cooled enough to be safe to handle, pour it into 25 sterile petri dishes and continue to cool to room temperature.

ADVANCE PREPARATIONS FOR PROTOCOL 7

NOTE: This protocol is similar to Protocol 6 but uses a different agar that is more conducive to growth of fungi rather than bacteria.

Sterilize the following materials, or provide sterile disposable equivalents where appropriate (quantities are per student group):

▶ 3 test tubes with caps

▶ 1 10-mL pipette

▶ 3 1-mL pipettes

▶ 3 0.1-mL pipettes

▶ 3 bacteriological spreading rods or cotton swabs

In addition, each student group will need:

▶ 72 mL phosphate buffer solution (sterile)

▶ 3 petri dishes containing PDA agar (sterile)

Preparing PDA Agar and Phosphate Buffer Solution

Materials

▶ 6.5 g potato dextrose agar

▶ 5.0 g bacto agar

▶ 500 mL distilled water in a 750 mL Erlenmeyer flask with foil cap

▶ 15 mg rifampicin

▶ 15 mg penicillin G

▶ 34 g KH_2PO_4

▶ 1000 mL distilled water in 1 L Erlenmeyer flask

▶ a few drops of NaOH or HCl (for pH adjustment)

▶ 1 250-mL Erlenmeyer flask with foil cap for each student group

Procedure

1. Make the PDA agar by mixing 6.5 g potato dextrose agar, 5.0 g bacto agar, and 500 mL distilled water in a 750 mL Erlenmeyer flask. Cover loosely with aluminum foil. (This makes enough to fill 25 petri dishes.)

2. Make phosphate buffer solution by mixing 34 g KH_2PO_4 into 1000 mL distilled water and then adjust the pH to 7. For each student group, measure 72 mL phosphate buffer solution into a 250 mL Erlenmeyer flask and cover with foil.

3. Sterilize the covered flasks containing PDA agar and phosphate buffer solutions for 20 minutes at 121°C in an autoclave or pressure cooker.

4. Cool the PDA agar solution until it is comfortable to handle, then add 15 mg rifampicin and penicillin G. (These antibiotics will help to limit growth of bacteria in these cultures.) Pour the mixture into sterile petri dishes and continue to cool to room temperature.

NOTES ABOUT PROTOCOL 8

Protocol 8 involves weighing the amount of CO_2 given off by a sample of soil or compost and then absorbed by a small amount of soda lime. Because the weight changes in the soda lime are quite small, this protocol requires a balance with a sensitivity of 0.01 g. The success of this protocol depends on very accurate, consistent weighing techniques. The more precise the balance and the more practiced the students are in its use, the better the outcome is likely to be.

If students do not have access to a precise balance but there is one available to teachers, you could carry out the weighing yourself but leave the rest of the protocol to the students. Similarly, if classroom time is a constraint, you could weigh the soda lime yourself to reduce the amount of class time needed for these steps.

Protocol 8 involves three steps: taking samples of soil or compost (Protocol 8a), measuring their moisture content (Protocol 8b), and then measuring the amount of CO_2 released over a 48-hour exposure period (Protocol 8c).

Protocol 8c can be scheduled over a five-day period, with recommended daily steps shown in Table 6.

TABLE 6
A Guide to Scheduling Protocol 8C

Day	Protocol Steps	Approximate Time Required*
1	**Part 3:** ▶ Weigh petri dish(es) and soda lime. ▶ Place soda lime in oven (if using a microwave, do this step on Day 2).	20–30 min.
2	**Part 2:** ▶ Mix soil samples. ▶ Weigh empty container. ▶ Spread soil sample in container and weigh. **Parts 1, 3, and 4:** ▶ Remove soda lime from oven and weigh it; place in soil (Part 4) and blank containers (Part 1). ▶ Seal containers and begin incubation.	30–40 min.
3	Nothing scheduled.	
4	**Part 4:** ▶ Open soil containers and remove soda lime. ▶ Place soda lime in oven.	10–15 min.
5	**Part 5:** ▶ Remove soda lime from oven and weigh.	20–30 min.

*These time estimates are based on analysis of five samples. The actual time required will vary depending on the number of samples and your level of familiarity with the protocol.

ADVANCE PREPARATIONS FOR PROTOCOL 10

Manganous Sulfate Solution

You can purchase manganous sulfate solution as "Winkler's Solution #1" (e.g., Flinn #W0005) or make it yourself:

Dissolve 480 g $MnSO_4 \bullet 4H_2O$ in 500 mL distilled water. Filter, then dilute to 1 L.

Alkaline Potassium Iodide Azide Solution

You can purchase alkaline potassium iodide azide solution as "Winkler's Solution #2" (e.g., Flinn #W0006) or make it yourself:

Dissolve 500 g NaOH and 150 g KI in 1 L distilled water. Dissolve 10 g NaN_3 in 40 mL distilled water. Combine these two solutions.

Sodium Thiosulfate Solution, 0.025 N

You can purchase sodium thiosulfate ($Na_2S_2O_3 \bullet 5H_2O$) as a 0.1 M solution (e.g., Flinn #S0402 or #S0150), then dilute to 0.025 M by mixing 250 mL 0.1 M solution with 750 mL distilled water.

Starch Indicator Solution

You can purchase starch indicator solution ready-made (e.g., Flinn #S0151) or make it yourself:

Mix 2 g soluble starch in 100 mL hot distilled water. Add 0.2 g salicylic acid to serve as a preservative.

ADVANCE PREPARATIONS FOR PROTOCOL 13

Sterilize the following materials, or provide sterile disposable equivalents where appropriate (quantities are per student group):

▶ 2 1-mL pipettes

▶ 5 0.1-mL pipettes

In addition, each student group will need:

▶ 2 250-mL flasks, each containing 100 mL distilled water (sterile)

▶ <1 mL of each of the following stock nutrient solutions (sterile):

$CaCl_2 \bullet 2H_2O$

$(NH4)_2HPO_4$

$MgSO_4 \bullet 7H_2O$

$FeCl_3 \bullet 6H_2O$

K_2HPO_4

Sterilizing Distilled Water

For each student group, measure 100 mL distilled water into each of two flasks and cover loosely with aluminum foil. Autoclave for 20 minutes and allow to cool.

Preparing Nutrient Stock Solutions

Materials

- 10 g $CaCl_2 \cdot 2H_2O$
- 10 g $(NH_4)_2HPO_4$
- 10 g $MgSO_4 \cdot 7H_2O$
- 10 g K_2HPO_4
- 1 g $FeCl_3 \cdot 6H_2O$
- 1 20-mL disposable syringe
- 1 syringe filter, 0.22-micron pore size (e.g., Cameo 25NS Nylon Filter from Fisher)
- 5 100-mL or larger jars with airtight lids
- 2 L distilled water

Procedure

1. Label each of the five jars with the name of one of the chemical compounds in the following table. Measure 100 mL distilled water into each jar, then make each into a nutrient stock solution by adding the specified amount of the designated compound:

Compound	Amount (g)	Distilled Water (mL)
$CaCl_2 \cdot 2H_2O$	10	100
$(NH_4)_2HPO_4$	10	100
$MgSO_4 \cdot 7H_2O$	10	100
K_2HPO_4	10	100
$FeCl_3 \cdot 6H_2O$	1	100

2. Sterilize the first four solutions for 20 minutes at 121°C in an autoclave or pressure cooker.

3. Filter-sterilize the $FeCl_3$ solution using a 20-mL disposable syringe to force the solution through the 0.22-micron filter and into a sterile bottle. (This solution should not be autoclaved because the heat and pressure cause it to become cloudy.)

ADVANCE PREPARATIONS FOR PROTOCOL 14

Preparing No-Carbon Agar

Materials

- 7.5 g noble agar
- 1.5 g trypticase soy broth

▶ 500 mL distilled water in 1 L Erlenmeyer flask with aluminum foil cap

▶ 4 1-mL pipettes (sterile)

▶ 1 10-mL pipette (sterile)

▶ 25 petri dishes (sterile)

Procedure

1. Wipe down your work area with disinfectant solution.

2. Mix 7.5 g noble agar into 500 mL distilled water in a 1 L Erlenmeyer flask.

3. Boil the solution, then cover loosely with foil.

4. Sterilize for 20 minutes at 121°C in an autoclave or pressure cooker.

5. When cool enough to handle safely, add the following quantities of salt stock solutions per liter distilled water:

Stock Solution	Amount (mL)
$CaCl_2 \cdot 2H_2O$	0.5
$MgSO_4 \cdot 7H_2O$	0.5
$FeCl_3 \cdot 6H_2O$	0.5
$(NH_4)_2HPO_4$	1.0
K_2HPO_4	4.0

6. Pour into sterile petri dishes, cover, and allow to cool.

INTERACTIVE RESEARCH:
EXPERIMENTS AND FIELD STUDIES

Biodegradation research provides a wealth of opportunities for student-designed experiments that are simple and inexpensive to perform and that address questions relevant to students and their communities. The following sequence of activities helps students to

▶ Develop research questions

▶ Carry out investigations

▶ Refine experimental design

▶ Continue with further experiments

Central to all these activities is the idea of communicating with fellow students through collaborative work and peer review.

WHY INTERACTIVE RESEARCH?

A common misconception among students is that scientists are social loners who work in isolation with little connection to each other or society. Through interactive research, students experience some of the ways in which professional scientists work together to discuss ideas, share findings, and collaborate on joint projects. In the process, they experience the following aspects of scientific inquiry and expand their understanding of the nature of science.

Scientists build on each other's work.

One of the elements of science that is difficult to replicate in high school classrooms is the idea that scientific investigation is a cumulative process, with each scientist learning from the work of both preceding and contemporary researchers. Before embarking on a new research endeavor, scientists typically begin by talking with colleagues, attending conferences, and reading related publications to learn what has already been accomplished and what questions remain unanswered.

The interactive research level of EI aims to provide analogous opportunities for high school students to base their research questions on what has already been learned in previous experiments. When time constraints make it impossible to carry out a series of experiments, students still can experience the cumulative and interactive aspects of research without having to carry out every step of the process themselves. For example, if you save student research reports from one year to the next, students can design their experiments based on results and recommendations made by previous student researchers, then conclude by making their own recommendations to next year's students. Rather than each class starting their research from square one, students model professional scientific practice by starting with an analysis of what has already been accomplished in the field. In carrying out these steps, students not only improve their understandings of their own research, they also gain a broader understanding of the ways in which scientists work both individually and collaboratively.

Research commonly begins with informal explorations.

Contrary to popular belief, scientists do not routinely launch into research by stating and then testing a hypothesis. In many cases, they start with a period of exploration, observation, and discovery that gradually leads to ideas about fruitful areas of investigation. If you can fit exploratory research into your class schedule, it will provide a chance for students to apply curiosity, imagination, and creativity to science rather than having to follow a predetermined set of rules. This period of trial and error also will help students to discover for themselves some of the basic principles of experimental design, such as the need for replicates and controls.

Based on considerations of curriculum, scheduling, and student ability levels, interactive research may consist of a single investigation or a series of iterations. Ideally, students carry out preliminary investigations, and then use the results of these explorations to reassess their focus and experimental design. They might decide to carry out additional exploratory level investigations or to use what they have learned to design a more rigorous experiment with a clearly defined hypothesis, dependent and independent variables, and replicates for each treatment.

Peer review is integral to science.

Professional scientists rely on peer review to separate fact from falsehood and good science from bad in the continuous search for new understandings about how the world works. Peer review also plays a key role in determining which research endeavors receive funding, which conference papers get accepted, and which articles get published in the most prestigious journals. Finally, peer review helps scientists to focus their thinking and improve their writing as they respond to comments from professional colleagues.

In schools, peer review of student research reports can provide similar opportunities for students to think critically as they question their own and each other's experimental designs, assumptions, results, interpretations, and conclusions. Peer review is an integral component of interactive research (Figure 2). After students have planned an experiment, they will benefit from meeting in pairs or small groups to discuss their ideas and exchange written feedback. A more formal type of peer review comes after students have completed their experiments. At this point, peer review provides a forum for critical evaluation of research results and helps students to improve the quality of their reports or poster presentations.

FIGURE 2
Peer Review in Interactive Research

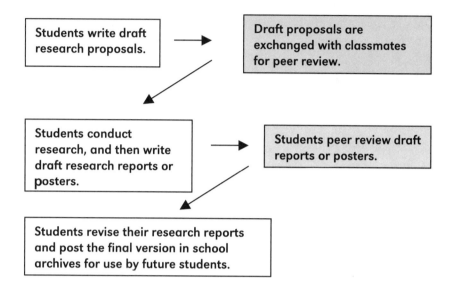

CHOOSING A RESEARCH QUESTION

The *Student Edition* includes protocols for carrying out studies on invertebrates, microorganisms, and water chemistry, as well as for constructing simple bioreactors for compost and landfill experiments. Based on their experience using one or more protocols, students will have ideas about interesting research questions on topics such as the following:

▶ Biodegradation in nature

▶ Factors influencing biodegradation in landfills and compost systems

▶ Physical, biological, and chemical aspects of wastewater treatment

▶ The role of microbes in bioremediation

▶ The influence of environmental conditions on breakdown of various substances, including biodegradable plastics

You might decide to give students wide leeway in choosing a topic and developing appropriate research questions and strategies. Or you might specify an overall topic, such as biodegradability of various plastics, then encourage each student group to develop individualized approaches to addressing relevant research questions.

To get students started in choosing research questions, one approach is to have the class collectively evaluate a poster or report produced by students in other classes or previous years. By reviewing completed projects, students will get ideas about interesting questions as well as effective research and presentation techniques.

The process of choosing a question and designing related investigations will be a new experience for students who are accustomed to traditional high school labs. Don't worry if your students initially seem frustrated with this assignment. After a period of floundering and hoping that you will help them to find the "right" answer, students will gain confidence and get accustomed to the idea of being responsible for open-ended inquiry. The EI student forms will help to focus student attention on the essential questions at each stage of the process:

▶ **Choosing a Research Topic** (p. 110) guides students through the process of choosing a research question that is both feasible and interesting.

▶ **Interactive Research Planning Form #1** (p. 113) helps in planning the logistics of exploratory-level experiments.

▶ **Interactive Research Planning Form #2** (p. 115) serves the same role for more rigorously designed experiments.

Figure 3 outlines some of the many interactive research topics that students can pursue using the biodegradation protocols.

ANALYZING THE DATA

"If the result confirms the hypothesis, then you've made a measurement. If the result is contrary to the hypothesis, then you've made a discovery."

—Enrico Fermi

When students are planning their own experiments, it is helpful for them to think about how they will organize and present the results. For example, they might start by labeling the columns and rows in a table or spreadsheet, indicating how they will summarize the data—for example, by calculating the mean of all replicates within a single treatment. Students also could begin by drawing an empty graph showing what independent variable will be portrayed on the x-axis and what dependent variable on the y-axis. It may seem premature to think about data analysis before conducting the experiment, but going through this process can help students to discover potential problems in their experimental designs before it is too late to make changes.

Choosing the Appropriate Type of Graph

The best way to decide on data analysis methods is to start by considering the specific research question being addressed. For example, analysis of whether trends are apparent over time requires a different sort of analysis than the question of whether one treatment is different from another or from the control. Students may be surprised to learn that different types of graphs are useful for different purposes. For analysis of trends over time, a line graph is appropriate. The lines connecting data points suggest predictions of values in-between the ones that have been measured. For example, a line graph is a useful way to portray changes in compost temperature over time (Figure 4).

FIGURE 3
From Protocols to Interactive Research

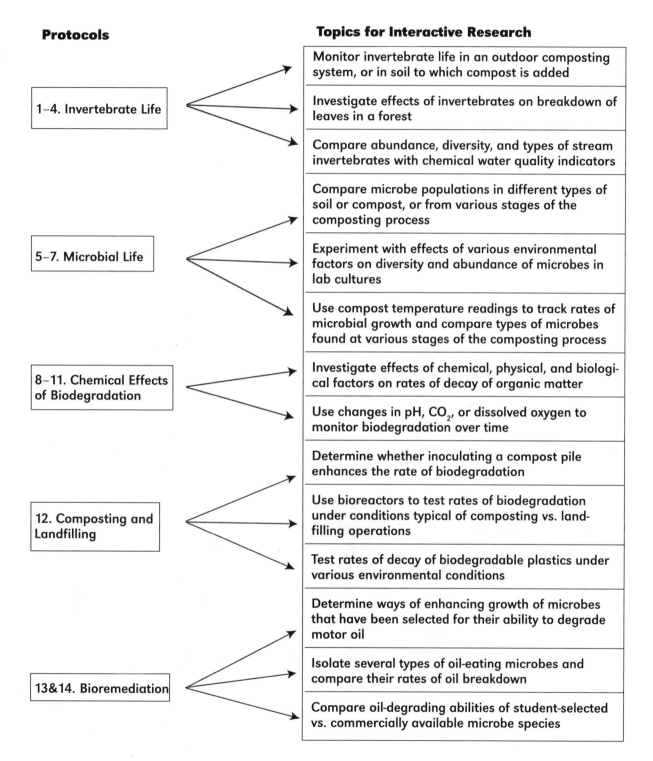

Protocols

Topics for Interactive Research

1–4. Invertebrate Life

- Monitor invertebrate life in an outdoor composting system, or in soil to which compost is added
- Investigate effects of invertebrates on breakdown of leaves in a forest
- Compare abundance, diversity, and types of stream invertebrates with chemical water quality indicators

5–7. Microbial Life

- Compare microbe populations in different types of soil or compost, or from various stages of the composting process
- Experiment with effects of various environmental factors on diversity and abundance of microbes in lab cultures
- Use compost temperature readings to track rates of microbial growth and compare types of microbes found at various stages of the composting process

8–11. Chemical Effects of Biodegradation

- Investigate effects of chemical, physical, and biological factors on rates of decay of organic matter
- Use changes in pH, CO_2, or dissolved oxygen to monitor biodegradation over time

12. Composting and Landfilling

- Determine whether inoculating a compost pile enhances the rate of biodegradation
- Use bioreactors to test rates of biodegradation under conditions typical of composting vs. land-filling operations
- Test rates of decay of biodegradable plastics under various environmental conditions

13&14. Bioremediation

- Determine ways of enhancing growth of microbes that have been selected for their ability to degrade motor oil
- Isolate several types of oil-eating microbes and compare their rates of oil breakdown
- Compare oil-degrading abilities of student-selected vs. commercially available microbe species

FIGURE 4
Line Graphs Show Trends over Time

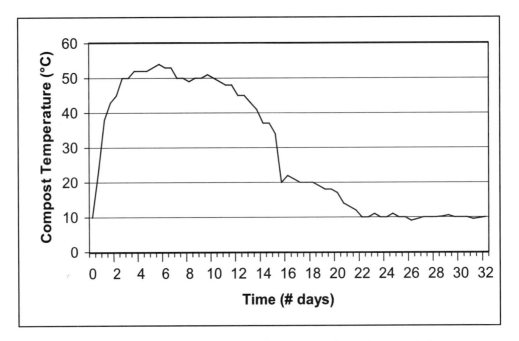

If there is no logical connection between data points, then a bar graph is more appropriate. This is the case when you are comparing two or more treatments (Figure 5).

FIGURE 5
Bar Graphs Show Differences between Treatment Means

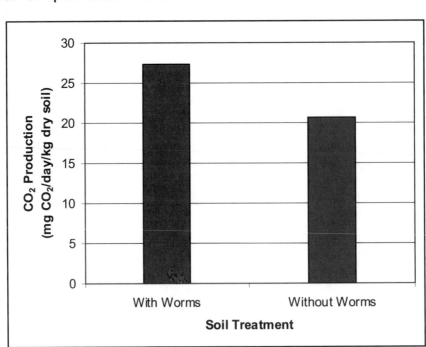

A LOOK AT VARIABILITY

A standard approach in analyzing research data is to look at the variability within each treatment compared with the variability between treatments. For example, if the data in Figure 5 are graphed as individual points rather than means, it becomes apparent that there is some overlap in values between the two treatments (Figure 6). This highlights the desirability of using replicates whenever feasible. In this case, one of the samples without worms actually generated more CO_2 than one of the samples with worms. If only these two samples had been used rather than three replicates of each treatment, the experimenter might have reached a different conclusion about the effect of worm respiration in this type of soil.

FIGURE 6
Graphs of Individual Data Points Show Variability within Each Treatment

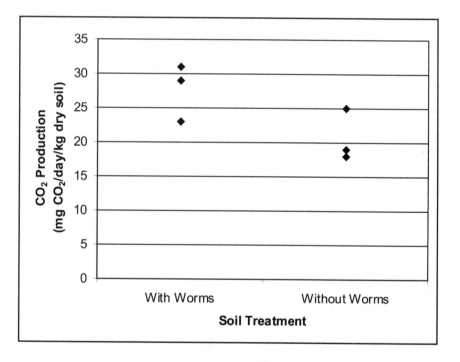

Students who are ready for a higher level of complexity can calculate standard deviations using scientific calculators or computer spreadsheet programs, then draw a bar representing ± one standard deviation around each mean (Figure 7). Standard deviation provides a measure of the degree of variability within the data collected for each treatment. The larger the standard deviation, the greater the spread between the individual data points making up the mean. Standard deviations therefore can be used to compare the variability within each treatment to the apparent differences between treatments. Students who have studied statistics may prefer to perform t-tests or an analysis of variance to calculate the statistical significance of apparent differences between treatments or between a treatment and the control.

FIGURE 7
Bar Graphs with ± 1 Standard Deviation, Another Way to Show Variability

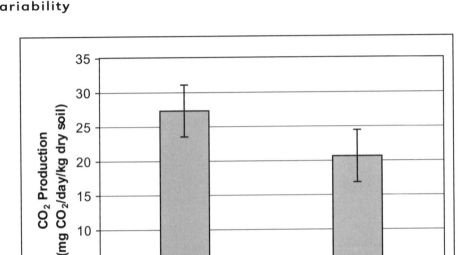

Some of the variability in data may be due to the fact that no matter how hard you try to mix the soil, the samples will not be identical. Similarly, there is unavoidable biological variability in the worms or other test organisms. However, in any experiment, there is some variability that can be controlled by the experimenter. Identifying these potential sources of variability will help students to figure out which types are unavoidable and which can be reduced through careful attention to detail.

INTERPRETING THE RESULTS

"The most exciting phrase to hear in science, the one that heralds new discoveries, is not 'Eureka!' (I found it!) but 'That's funny ....'"

—Isaac Asimov

After students have summarized their data, they will be ready to try to figure out what conclusions they can reach. A common misconception among students is that experiments should always reveal definitive answers to the research question. In reality, many experiments only partially answer the original question, and often the question changes as the research proceeds through several rounds of experiments. Perhaps the original question was not narrowly enough defined, or the methods were inadequate. Or perhaps everything went according to plan, but more trials are needed before conclusions can be reached.

It is important for students to recognize that they have not failed if their experiment didn't work out as expected. In fact, sometimes the most unexpected results lead to the most interesting discoveries. The results of an experiment, even when seemingly ambiguous or contradictory, often lead to new insights, new questions, and new investigations. Scientific research rarely ends with definitive answers—more commonly, the results of each experiment suggest ideas for further studies. If students have learned something from their experiment, then it was a success. The important thing is for them to evaluate their findings at each stage of the process and to apply what they have learned to decisions about next steps. Even if they will not be carrying out further experiments themselves, they can make recommendations for future students.

PRESENTING A REPORT AND ENGAGING IN PEER REVIEW

The final step in research is to communicate the findings in a way that can be understood and used by others. When students present their research findings, they can benefit from presenting to an audience rather than just turning in a report for a grade. The **Research Report Peer Review Form** (p. 125) and **Poster Peer Review Form** (p. 126) provide examples that you can adapt for student level and types of presentations used. Alternatively, you might choose to work with your students to devise your own peer review form based on criteria such as those listed in the **Assessment Criteria for Student Research** (*Teacher Edition*, p. 44).

> Public discussion of the explanations proposed by students is a form of peer review of investigations, and peer review is an important aspect of science. Talking with peers about science experiences helps students develop meaning and understanding. Their conversations clarify the concepts and processes of science, helping students make sense of the content of science.[3]

After exchanging peer reviews, students should be encouraged to consider using this feedback to revise their research reports. To assess their understanding of the peer review process, you might ask them to address questions such as the following in their final write-ups:

▶ What peer review comments did you receive?

▶ Did you agree with these comments? Why or why not?

▶ How did you use the comments in preparing your final report?

Inevitably, some of your students will receive peer reviews that are not helpful, possibly even tactless or otherwise inappropriate. A classroom discussion about this problem can be used to point out that such weaknesses can occur in professional scientific review as well, but the goal for all peer reviewers should be to provide constructive criticism in order to promote better science.

---

[3] National Research Council (NRC). 1996. *National Science Education Standards*. Washington, DC: National Academy Press, p. 174.

INTERACTIVE RESEARCH:
WASTEWATER TREATMENT DESIGN CHALLENGE

In this technological design project, students work in teams to design and test a system for wastewater treatment involving a combination of physical, biological, and chemical steps that must be optimized while minimizing costs. Experiences such as this help students to realize the need to integrate mathematical analysis, scientific inquiry, and technological design in making informed decisions and solving real-world problems.

Participating in a technological design project requires that students gather and process information, generate and analyze ideas, present results, and probably most difficult of all, get practice working effectively in teams. One of the benefits of this teamwork is that students learn firsthand the value of skills in conceptualization, design, and construction. The team members who come up with the most creative design solutions often are not the same ones who perform best at book learning.

MAKING SYNTHETIC WASTEWATER

For the purposes of this design challenge, you want to provide your students with wastewater that is safe to handle and contains solids, dissolved organic matter, and nutrients. You can create this by mixing the following ingredients into tap water:

- soil or potting soil—provides solid particles and suspended sediments (use ~10 g/L)

- vermiculite or foam beads—provides floating particles (use ~1 g/L)

- cornstarch—provides dissolved and suspended organic matter (use ~10 g/L)

- houseplant fertilizer—provides nutrients (use the concentration recommended for houseplants)

This combination creates a wastewater that can be treated in many ways, including physical processes to remove solids, and biological and chemical processes to reduce the concentrations of dissolved organic matter and nutrients.

SUMMARY OF THE STEPS

Step 1. Define the Problem

The first step introduces the students to the scenario and to basic concepts in wastewater treatment. It also begins their progression through the problem-solving cycle by having them state the problem in their own words and begin to think about design possibilities.

At this stage, you should discuss with the class what tests they will be using to determine the quality of the effluent from their treatment units. Ideally, you'll want to be able to measure turbidity, biological oxygen demand, and concentrations of nitrate, ammonia-N, and phosphate. For turbidity, you can measure light dispersal in a spectrophotometer, use a turbidity test kit, or devise some other method of comparing clarity of the samples. Protocol 9 describes how to measure biological oxygen demand. Nitrate, ammonia-N, and phosphate can be measured using test kits or probes. Deciding upfront which water quality parameters will be measured following treatment will help students to tailor their designs to the most relevant variables.

Step 2. Identify Alternative Design Solutions and Select the Best Alternative

In Step 2, students brainstorm various design ideas. Each team of students should generate at least two design options based on the requirements specified in the problem. The *Student Edition* contains a parts list with prices, which students can use in selecting parts and working to optimize their design ideas. Many students may choose to manipulate the materials to get a feel for what will work. That's OK, but the emphasis at this point is on coming up with design ideas rather than on constructing the treatment unit. Students may have ideas about parts not included on the list. If so, you will need to set the rules about what types of materials will be allowed and what the prices will be.

Step 3. Select the Best Alternative

This step provides a systematic approach to selecting the best design. Although "best" sounds absolute, there is no single right answer to the design challenge, and each group is likely to come up with a different plan. Ideally the student teams will build and test a wide variety of devices based on their understandings of physical, biological, and chemical aspects of wastewater treatment.

In order to select the best alternative, students must determine how well each of their design ideas meets the specifications and restrictions posed by the problem. Trade-offs will be necessary—that's part of the design process. In order to systematically analyze their options and decide among some of these trade-offs, students will create a qualitative or quantitative assessment scale. The **Design Selection Rubric** included in the *Student Edition* (p. 137) is intended to serve as an example that the students can adapt to meet their own specific needs. Once each team has selected their best design alternative, they can use the **Design Proposal Form** (p. 138) to present their ideas to you for approval before they begin construction. This form asks specific questions regarding physical, chemical, and biological treatment in order to trigger students' thinking about what they are trying to accomplish and how this fits with what they have learned about the science of wastewater treatment.

Step 4. Build and Test the Best Design

Students will construct and test their wastewater treatment system using selected items from the parts list and any other materials you have decided to approve. As students assemble their system, they will need to test it at various stages of development. Testing over lab sinks works best in case the devices spring leaks or do not function as planned.

Students may find it necessary to make modifications in their designs to overcome problems such as leaks or treatment constraints. That's fine—you can point out that design should be an iterative process, with continuous improvements based on experience. Students should keep track of these changes and be prepared to discuss what modifications they made and why. If they decide to make major design changes, they may need to go back and reapply the methods from Step 3 for judging alternative choices.

Step 5. Evaluate the Constructed System

When students have completed the construction and testing of their model, the next step is to assess how well it has worked. How you do this depends on what lab facilities, test kits, or probes you have available.

The **Design Challenge Peer Review Form** (p. 140) guides students through systematic assessment of the quality of their work. At this stage, they can use it to evaluate their own systems, and later they will use it to critique other groups' work. The rubric includes a weighting column so that some criteria can be given greater weight than others in the scoring process. You could announce the weights or have the class participate in assigning them. You may want to help students to develop guidelines for each of the five evaluation scores, specifying the minimum requirements for success for each of the criteria.

Step 6. Plan a Presentation

Students will have spent a great deal of time planning, designing, and building their wastewater treatment system to meet the required specifications. It is important for them to realize that in the workplace, their project isn't complete until they have presented their results. Design challenge results can be presented using the actual wastewater treatment devices as props, or using posters or computerized presentation software. Students should use their presentations to demonstrate their knowledge of wastewater treatment principles and to provide their perspectives on how well their treatment system worked. If things didn't work as well as they had expected, that's fine as long as they provide a good explanation of what happened and what they would do differently next time. Students can use the **Design Challenge Peer Review Form** (p. 140) as a checklist to make sure that their presentation will cover all the important points.

Step 7. Present Your Work

If possible, make the design challenge into a competition, with the winners selected through student peer review. This helps students to take the peer review process seriously and to realize that they can make valuable contributions to the assessment process. A copy of the **Design Challenge Peer Review Form** (p. 140) should be provided to each student for assessment of each presentation. You may want to meet with each team after the presentations are completed to review the results of the self-assessment, peer-assessment, and teacher assessment. This will give them essential feedback and help them to learn from their design, construction, and presentation experiences.

ASSESSMENT

PERFORMANCE ASSESSMENT

Although sample test questions are included on pages 48–53, student performance in EI research is best assessed using the collections of worksheets and other written records assembled by students as they go through the processes of designing and conducting experiments, interpreting and presenting results, and engaging in peer review.

In assessing student research, clearly defined "right" or "wrong" answers rarely exist. Instead, the goal of assessment is to evaluate the process used by the students and the conceptual understandings they have achieved through their research experiences. Laboratory journals, worksheets, draft reports, and responses to peer review all will provide evidence of the progress that students have made in thinking critically, synthesizing information, and carrying out scientific research. The following pages outline possible assessment criteria for student research, as well as example assessment rubrics for posters and written reports. These can be downloaded in electronic form from the EI website *(http://ei.cornell.edu)* so that you can make adaptations to meet the needs of your particular students and their projects.

The peer review process provides both opportunities and challenges for assessment. Through peer review, some of the assessment responsibility can be shifted from the teacher to the students themselves—an important step in promoting self-regulated learning. Once students become familiar with peer review, they may become motivated to work harder and to look more critically at their own work because they begin to anticipate the expectations of other students carrying out projects similar to their own.

Since it probably will be too cumbersome to keep track of all the comments exchanged by students, we suggest you concentrate on determining how students respond to the feedback they receive. This approach helps to overcome any worries among students about whether it is fair to be evaluated by someone other than their teacher. If they don't agree with reviewers' suggestions, that's fine as long as they can justify their position. In their final research reports, you can direct students to summarize the comments they received from peer reviewers, whether they agreed with these critiques, and how they used them in revising their work.

EXAMPLE ASSESSMENT RUBRICS FOR EI STUDENT RESEARCH

Assessment Criteria for Student Research

Criteria such as these can be used to create a checklist for students and a grading rubric for completed research portfolios.

Identify a Researchable Question

❏ Develop a researchable question, including a clear statement of why this question is relevant to biodegradation.

❏ Review previous work in the field, including Internet as well as print sources.

❏ Formulate a hypothesis that addresses the research question, and predict experimental results.

Plan the Investigation

❏ Identify treatments and a control.

❏ Plan to vary only one independent variable at a time.

❏ Plan adequate replicates of each treatment.

❏ Describe appropriate tools and techniques to gather, interpret, and analyze the data within constraints of time and resources.

❏ Identify safety concerns and precautions that will be taken.

Conduct the Research

❏ Carry out one or a series of experiments, using proper equipment and safety precautions.

❏ Record data and observations at appropriate intervals.

❏ Document any decisions made about experimental design or data collection as the experiment progresses.

Analyze the Data

❏ Summarize data clearly using tables and graphs.

❏ Identify trends and outlying data that do not fit the trends.

❏ Identify potential sources of variability.

Interpret the Results and Formulate Conclusions

❏ Compare actual results to predicted results.

❏ Clearly state the meaning of the results in terms of the original research question.

❏ Identify possible improvements in the experimental design.

❏ Suggest new directions for future research.

Present the Project and Engage in Peer Review

❏ Effectively communicate the experimental design and results to a peer audience.

❏ Defend or revise conclusions based on consideration of alternative explanations of research results.

❏ Revise written report or poster presentation when appropriate based on reviewers' comments.

Assessment Rubrics for Poster Presentations

Name(s) of student(s) _____

Date _____

ASSESSMENT SCALE
1—Inadequate in meeting requirements of the task
2—Minimal in meeting requirements of the task
3—Adequate in meeting requirements of the task
4—Superior in meeting requirements of the task

Poster Presentation Criteria	Evaluation	Points
The poster includes these sections: Title, Research Question, Hypothesis, Procedure, Results, Conclusions, and Acknowledgments (if appropriate)	1 2 3 4	
The purpose is clearly stated in the research question and hypothesis.	1 2 3 4	
The procedure is described clearly enough to be reproduced.	1 2 3 4	
Results and conclusions are displayed in a sequence that is easy to follow.	1 2 3 4	
The display is neat, clearly labeled, and easy to read.	1 2 3 4	
The ideas fit together and make sense.	1 2 3 4	

Comments: **TOTAL**

ASSESSMENT SCALE
"?" = Not enough information available to evaluate this question.
Assign 5 points for each "Yes" and 0 points for each "No" or "?".

Experimental Design Criteria	Evaluation	Points
The experiment was appropriately designed to test the stated hypothesis.	Yes No ?	
Only one independent variable was changed at a time.	Yes No ?	
There was a control, which was exposed to the same conditions as the treatments except for the independent variable.	Yes No ?	
Adequate replicates were provided for each treatment.	Yes No ?	
The conclusions appear well supported by the data.	Yes No ?	

Comments: **TOTAL**

Assessment Rubric for Written Reports

Name(s) of student(s) _____

Date _____

ASSESSMENT SCALE

1—Inadequate in meeting requirements of the task

2—Minimal in meeting requirements of the task

3—Adequate in meeting requirements of the task

4—Superior in meeting requirements of the task

Criteria	Evaluation	Points
Introduction		
States a researchable question, and clearly explains why this question is relevant to biodegradation.	1 2 3 4	
Summarizes previous work in the field, if applicable.	1 2 3 4	
States a hypothesis that addresses the research question and expected results.	1 2 3 4	
Procedure		
Experiment is appropriately designed to address the research question.	1 2 3 4	
Describes procedures clearly enough to be replicated.	1 2 3 4	
Includes independent and dependent variables and a control.	1 2 3 4	
Changes only one independent variable between treatments.	1 2 3 4	
Provides adequate replicates of each treatment.	1 2 3 4	
Uses proper equipment, techniques, and safety precautions.	1 2 3 4	
Includes data and observations recorded at appropriate intervals.	1 2 3 4	
Results		
Summarizes data clearly using tables and graphs.	1 2 3 4	
Identifies trends and outlying data.	1 2 3 4	
Discusses potential sources of variability.	1 2 3 4	

Conclusions		
Compares actual results to predicted results.	1 2 3 4	
Clearly discusses meaning of the results in terms of the original research question.	1 2 3 4	
Makes conclusions that are well supported by the data.	1 2 3 4	
Identifies possible improvements in the experimental design.	1 2 3 4	
Suggests new directions for future research.	1 2 3 4	
Defends or revises conclusions based on consideration of alternative explanations of research results.	1 2 3 4	
Overall Report		
Displays understanding of experimental design.	1 2 3 4	
Displays understanding of applicable concepts in biodegradation.	1 2 3 4	
Includes clear discussion of use of peer review comments in revising the research report, or logical argument for why peer suggestions were not followed.	1 2 3 4	
Appropriately cites written and/or Internet references.	1 2 3 4	
Is neat, organized, and well written.	1 2 3 4	
Organizes ideas clearly.	1 2 3 4	
Uses proper spelling and grammar.	1 2 3 4	
	TOTAL	

SAMPLE TEST QUESTIONS

A student designed an experiment to investigate biodegradation of leaves in a forest. She weighed 50 grams of leaves into each of four mesh bags—two bags with a large mesh size and the other two with a smaller mesh. She buried the bags under the leaves at the surface of the soil in the woods next to her school. After leaving the bags buried for one month, she dug them up and then dried and weighed the contents. She recorded her data in the following table.

Bag #	Dry Weight of Leaves in 10 mm Mesh Bags	Dry Weight of Leaves in 0.01 mm Mesh Bags
1	23 g	
2	19 g	
3		38 g
4		35 g

1. What would be a good hypothesis for this experiment?

   a. Leaves degrade faster if they are buried more deeply in the soil.

   b. Mesh bags prevent leaves from degrading in forest soil.

   c. Moisture is important in biodegradation of leaves in forest soil.

   d. *Leaves degrade faster in the presence of worms and other large soil invertebrates.*

2. What would you conclude from the data that this student obtained?

   a. There was more moisture in bags 1 and 2.

   b. *Worms and other large invertebrates may have helped to degrade the leaves in bags 1 and 2.*

   c. There was more moisture in bags 3 and 4.

   d. Worms and other large invertebrates helped to degrade the leaves in bags 3 and 4.

3. If you wanted to create a self-sustaining ecosystem in a sealed jar, what types of organisms would you add, and why?

   Green plants, at least one type of consumer to eat the plants, and a source of bacteria and fungi to carry out decomposition and make nutrients available for new growth.

4. What do composting, bioremediation, and wastewater treatment all have in common?

   These three processes are designed to accelerate natural processes of decay and renewal in order to protect or improve environmental quality. All three depend on microorganisms to break down organic matter or pollutant chemicals as they use these materials for food.

5. Suppose that you get hot when you go running. What does this have in common with compost getting hot if it is made with the right mix of ingredients?

   a. Both are caused by cellular respiration.

   b. Both depend on trapping heat from the sun.

   c. Both are examples of biodegradation.

   d. Both occur only when the weather is hot.

6. Why are green plants needed by most organisms, including decomposers?

   a. They convert solar energy into chemical energy.

   b. They produce carbon dioxide.

   c. They help to cycle nutrients through ecosystems.

   d. They carry out respiration.

7. The key scientific principle behind bioremediation is that:

   a. Environmental contaminants tend to be toxic to microorganisms.

   b. Some microbes can use contaminants as a source of carbon and energy.

   c. Some contaminants can be biodegraded in landfills.

   d. Soil invertebrates can be used to clean up pollution.

8. Which of the following are needed for biodegradation to occur?

   a. Microbes

   b. Moisture

   c. Carbon

   d. All of the above

9. The primary reason why biodegradation occurs more rapidly in compost than in landfills is because:

   a. There are more bacteria and fungi in landfills.

   b. Bacteria and fungi grow best with adequate moisture, nutrients, and oxygen.

   c. The airflow is better in landfills.

   d. Compost piles have more worms and other invertebrates.

10. In a pond ecosystem, there are fish, turtles, frogs, and various plants such as duckweed and water lilies. The energy that supports this ecosystem comes from:

    a. Consumers

    b. Sunlight

    c. The water

    d. Decomposers

11. What types of organisms carry out cellular respiration?

    a. Producers

    b. Consumers

    c. Decomposers

    d. All of the above

12. A student measured dissolved oxygen in a pond each hour, and made the following graph. During what period of day or night was she sampling? How can you tell?

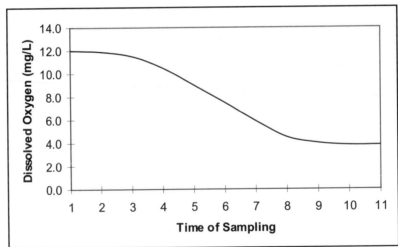

She was sampling during the afternoon and evening. The dissolved oxygen level drops because photosynthesis stops when the sun goes down but respiration by plants, animals, and microbes continues to use oxygen through the night as well as the day.

13. In this energy pyramid, which level represents producers?

   a. The top level

   b. The 2nd level down from the top

   c. The 3rd level down from the top

   d. The bottom level

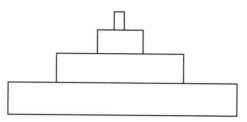

14. Decomposers are important in a pond because they:

   a. Help to achieve a balance between producers and consumers.

   b. Make nutrients available to other organisms.

   c. Help to prevent eutrophication.

   d. Complete the energy cycle.

15. An energy pyramid gets smaller toward the top because:

   a. Decomposers eat some of the organic matter at each level.

   b. There are more consumers than producers.

   c. Energy cycles from producers to consumers and back again.

   d. Much of the chemical energy at each level is lost as heat.

16. What process is represented by this equation:

   glucose + oxygen $\longrightarrow$ carbon dioxide + water + energy

   a. Respiration

   b. Photosynthesis

   c. Bioremediation

   d. Predation

17. A green plant was placed in an airtight jar on a sunny windowsill. By the end of the day, which of the following is likely to have occurred?

    a. The plant will have produced carbon dioxide through photosynthesis.

    b. The plant will have run out of oxygen and died.

    c. The concentration of carbon dioxide inside the jar will have decreased.

    d. The concentration of carbon dioxide inside the jar will not have changed.

18. When a tree dies and decays, where would you expect to find the carbon that used to be in its cells?

    a. In the bodies of forest insects, animals, and other organisms

    b. In the air

    c. In soil and water

    d. All of the above

19. What type of organism must be at the beginning of every food chain?

    a. Producer

    b. Consumer

    c. Decomposer

    d. Microorganism

20. What do producers, consumers, and decomposers all have in common?

    a. They all produce food.

    b. They all produce oxygen.

    c. They all produce carbon dioxide.

    d. None of the above.

		True or False:
T	(F)	Only organisms with lungs or gills can carry out cellular respiration.
T	(F)	Plants carry out respiration only in the dark.
(T)	F	Scientific explanations of natural processes can change based on new evidence.
T	(F)	The world would be a safer place if we could get rid of all microorganisms.
(T)	F	Cellular respiration is the process through which all types of organisms use the energy that is stored in chemicals such as glucose.
(T)	F	Carbon dioxide is produced as a waste product during respiration.
(T)	F	Carbon cycles between living and nonliving forms but is not created or destroyed in ecosystems.
(T)	F	If the Earth stopped receiving energy from the Sun, decomposers would run out of things to eat.
(T)	F	At each link in a food chain or food web, much of the available energy is lost as heat.
T	(F)	Consumers depend on producers, but they could live without decomposers.
(T)	F	Streams with good water quality can support organisms that need high levels of dissolved oxygen.
(T)	F	Wastewater treatment makes use of processes that also occur in nature.
T	(F)	You would expect to find low diversity of species in a stream with high water quality.

REFERENCES

BIODEGRADATION

Adams, D.L. 1999. Issues-directed chemistry: Teaching chemical reactions using waste treatment. *Journal of Chemical Education* 76(8): 1088-1091.

Coyne, M. 1999. *Soil Microbiology: An Exploratory Approach.* Albany, NY: Delmar.

Doberski, J. 1998. Teaching ecology through wastewater treatment. *Journal of Biological Education* 32(3): 216-225.

Hudler, G. 1998. *Magical Mushrooms, Mischievous Molds.* Princeton, NJ: Princeton University Press.

Rathje, W.L., and C. Murphy. 1992. *Rubbish! The Archaeology of Garbage.* New York: HarperCollins.

Soil and Water Conservation Society. 2000. *Soil Biology Primer.* Ankeny, IA: Soil and Water Conservation Society, *http://www.swcs.org.*

Trautmann, N.M., and M.E. Krasny. 1998. *Composting in the Classroom: Scientific Inquiry for High School Students.* Dubuque, IA: Kendall/Hunt. ISBN 0-7872-4433-3.

BIOREMEDIATION

U.S. Environmental Protection Agency. 1993. *Bioremediation: Innovative Pollution Treatment Technology: A Focus on EPA's Research.* EPA 640/K-93/002. Washington, DC: U.S. EPA, Office of Research and Development.

U.S. Environmental Protection Agency. 1997. *Compost—New Applications for an Age-Old Technology.* EPA 530-F-97-047. Washington, DC: U.S. EPA, Solid Waste and Emergency Response Division.

U.S. Environmental Protection Agency. 1998. *An Analysis of Composting as an Environmental Remediation Technology.* EPA 530-R-98-008. Washington, DC: U.S. EPA, Solid Waste and Emergency Response Division.

OIL SPILLS

U.S. Congress, Office of Technology Assessment. 1991. *Bioremediation for Marine Oil Spills—Background Paper.* OTA-BP-0-70. Washington, DC: U.S. Government Printing Office.

U.S. Environmental Protection Agency. 1993. *Understanding Oil Spills and Oil Spill Responses.* EPA 540-K-93-003. Washington, DC: U.S. EPA, Emergency Response Division.

Wright, R.G. 1995. *Oil Spill! An Event-Based Science Module.* Parsippany, NJ: Dale Seymour. ISBN 0-201-49090-0.

INQUIRY-BASED SCIENCE

Cothron, J.H., R.N. Giese, and R.J. Rezba. 1999. *Students and Research, 3rd ed.* Dubuque, IA: Kendall/Hunt. ISBN 0-7872-6478-4.

Doran, R., F. Chan, P. Tamir, and C. Lenhardt. 2002. *Science Educator's Guide to Laboratory Assessment.* Arlington, VA: NSTA Press. ISBN 0-87355-210-5.

Driver, R., A. Squires, P. Rushworth, and V. Wood-Robinson. 1994. *Making Sense of Secondary Science: Research into Children's Ideas.* London: Routledge.

National Research Council. 1996. *National Science Education Standards.* Washington, DC: National Academy Press. ISBN 0-309-05326-9.

National Research Council. 2000. *Inquiry and the National Science Education Standards.* Washington, DC: National Academy Press. ISBN 0-309-06476-7.

Thayer School of Engineering. 1993. *Engineering Problem Solving in the High School Classroom.* Dartmouth College. *http://thayer.dartmouth.edu/~teps/.*

OTHER BOOKS IN THE CORNELL SCIENTIFIC INQUIRY SERIES

Krasny, M.E., and the Environmental Inquiry Team. 2002. *Invasion Ecology, Student Edition and Teacher's Guide.* Arlington, VA: NSTA Press.

Trautmann, N.M., and the Environmental Inquiry Team. 2001. *Assessing Toxic Risk, Student Edition and Teacher's Guide.* Arlington, VA: NSTA Press.

CONTACT INFORMATION FOR SCIENTIFIC SUPPLY COMPANIES

The following companies are referred to in *Decay and Renewal:*

Fisher Scientific
http://www.fishersci.com/
800-766-7000

Flinn Scientific
http://www.flinnsci.com/
800-452-1261

Hach Company
http://www.hach.com/
800-227-4224

LaMotte Company
http://www.lamotte.com/
800-344-3100

Ward's Natural Science
http://www.wardsci.com/
800-962-2660

NOTES

NOTES

NOTES

NOTES

NOTES

CORNELL SCIENTIFIC INQUIRY SERIES
STUDENT EDITION

Decay and Renewal

NSTApress®
NATIONAL SCIENCE TEACHERS ASSOCIATION

CORNELL SCIENTIFIC INQUIRY SERIES

STUDENT EDITION

Decay and Renewal

BY THE ENVIRONMENTAL INQUIRY LEADERSHIP TEAM
NANCY M. TRAUTMANN
MARIANNE E. KRASNY
WILLIAM S. CARLSEN
CHRISTINE M. CUNNINGHAM

WITH TEACHERS
HARRY CANNING (NEWARK VALLEY HIGH SCHOOL)
PATRICIA CARROLL (NEWARK VALLEY HIGH SCHOOL)
MARK JOHNSON (ITHACA HIGH SCHOOL)
ALPA KHANDAR (HILTON HIGH SCHOOL)
ELAINA OLYNCIW (A. PHILIP RANDOLPH HIGH SCHOOL)

AND CORNELL SCIENTISTS
BENNETT KOTTLER
STEPHEN PENNINGROTH
ADAM WELMAN

NSTApress®
NATIONAL SCIENCE TEACHERS ASSOCIATION
Arlington, Virginia

NATIONAL SCIENCE TEACHERS ASSOCIATION

Claire Reinburg, Director

J. Andrew Cocke, Associate Editor

Judy Cusick, Associate Editor

Betty Smith, Associate Editor

ART AND DESIGN Linda Olliver, Director

   Cover image ©Russell Illig/Getty Images.

   Illustrations by Jane MacDonald of Sunset Design and Lucy Gagliardo.

PRINTING AND PRODUCTION Catherine Lorrain-Hale, Director

   Nguyet Tran, Assistant Production Manager

   Jack Parker, Desktop Publishing Specialist

PUBLICATIONS OPERATIONS Hank Janowsky, Manager

MARKETING Holly Hemphill, Director

NSTA WEB Tim Weber, Webmaster

PERIODICALS PUBLISHING Shelley Carey, Director

sciLINKS Tyson Brown, Manager

   David Anderson, Web and Development Coordinator

NATIONAL SCIENCE TEACHERS ASSOCIATION

Gerald F. Wheeler, Executive Director

David Beacom, Publisher

Decay and Renewal
NSTA Stock Number: PB162X3S
ISBN: 0-87355-212-1
05 04 03 4 3 2 1
Printed on recycled paper

Library of Congress Cataloging-in-Publication Data
Trautmann, Nancy M.
   Decay and renewal / by Nancy M. Trautmann and the Environmental
Inquiry Leadership Team.— Student ed.
   p. cm. — (Cornell scientific inquiry series)
ISBN 0-87355-212-1
1. Biodegradation—Research. 2. Bioremediation—Research.
I. National Science Teachers Association. Environmental Inquiry Leadership
Team. II. Title. III. Series.
QH530.5.T73 2003
577'.1—dc21   2003001325

This material is based on the work supported by the National Science Foundation under Grant No. 96-18142. Any opinions, findings, conclusions, or recommendations expressed in this material are those of the authors and do not necessarily reflect the views of the National Science Foundation.

Contents

STUDENT EDITION

Section 2. Biodegradation Protocols: Introduction to Research

Section 3. Interactive Research: Experiments and Field Studies

SECTION 4. INTERACTIVE RESEARCH: WASTEWATER TREATMENT DESIGN CHALLENGE

FIGURES AND TABLES IN THE *STUDENT EDITION*

PREFACE

WHY STUDY DECAY AND RENEWAL?

When you throw something away or flush it down the drain, you probably don't stop to think about where it is going and what will become of it—it just goes away. In the big picture, of course, there is no "away." Some substances will break down and others will not, and either way leads to environmental consequences. Although we don't often stop to think about it, our quality of life depends on the natural forces of decay and renewal that break down organic materials and recycle nutrients back into forms that can support new life.

Humans use these natural forces of decay and renewal in systems that are designed to prevent or clean up pollution. For example, compost systems are designed to support rapid growth of bacteria and fungi that decompose food scraps and other organic wastes. Similarly, wastewater treatment systems use decomposer microbes to break down organic wastes before the water is released into a river, lake, or ocean. And when oil washes up on beaches after an oil spill at sea, one way of cleaning it up is to apply fertilizer in order to stimulate growth of bacteria and fungi that can use oil as a source of food. All of these processes rely on providing environmental conditions that will stimulate rapid growth of decomposer microbes.

CARRYING OUT YOUR OWN RESEARCH

This book is part of the Environmental Inquiry series developed at Cornell University to enable you to conduct environmental science research on topics that relate to you and your community. Using the research protocols in this book, you will be equipped to carry out experiments on biodegradation in nature and in human-engineered systems for composting, wastewater treatment, or cleaning up pollution such as oil spills.

We hope that your research experiences will lead to some interesting discoveries. You may find yourself coming up with new questions and uncertainties rather than with concrete answers. Don't worry—that is the way science works! One of the things that make science exciting is that it is a continuous process of discovery, and there is always more to be learned.

HOW TO USE THIS BOOK

This book is designed to help you design and conduct your own experiments and also to experience some of the ways in which scientists work together to discuss ideas, exchange feedback, and collaborate on joint projects.

Section 1 provides background information about biodegradation of organic materials in nature and the ways in which humans harness these natural processes to prevent or clean up pollution. The next section presents 14 research protocols. Using one or more of these protocols, you will be able to design and carry out your own experiments. Section 3 provides advice to help you choose from a wide range of ideas for research projects, and a series of worksheets designed to guide your progress through the various steps of designing and carrying out an experiment, presenting your results, and exchanging feedback with fellow students. Section 4 gives step-by-step directions for an engineering design challenge related to wastewater treatment.

As you make your way through your research and engineering design projects, we encourage you to visit our website (*http://ei.cornell.edu*) to find online resources and to share your experiences, observations, and questions with other participating students. Have fun, and good luck with your research!

—Nancy Trautmann
Lead Author

How can you avoid searching hundreds of science websites to locate the best sources of information on a given topic? SciLinks, created and maintained by the National Science Teachers Association (NSTA), has the answer.

In a SciLinked text, such as this one, you'll find a logo and keyword near a concept your class is studying, a URL (*www.scilinks.org*), and a keyword code. Simply go to the SciLinks website, type in the code, and receive an annotated listing of as many as 15 web pages—all of which have gone through an extensive review process conducted by a team of science educators. SciLinks is your best source of pertinent, trustworthy Internet links on subjects from astronomy to zoology.

Need more information? Take a tour—*http://www.scilinks.org/tour/*

UNDERSTANDING BIODEGRADATION

CHAPTER 1

NATURAL FORCES OF DECAY AND RENEWAL

BIODEGRADATION

When a tree dies in the wilderness, there is no natural force that hauls it off to a landfill. Instead, the dead tree slowly decays. Woodpeckers make holes in their search for beetles and other insects that tunnel their way through the dead wood. Bacteria, fungi, and a wide variety of insects and other invertebrates feed on the wood, gradually breaking it down. As the trunk becomes hollow, it provides shelter for owls, raccoons, chipmunks, and many other forms of wildlife. Eventually, the tree falls, and the cycle of decay continues until the wood crumbles and blends in with the surrounding soil.

What would happen if this natural process of decay did not take place? Piles of dead plants and animals would cover the earth. Each year, as leaves fell and plants and animals reached the ends of their lives, the piles would become deeper until nothing more could grow. Eventually, the chemicals needed for life would be tied up in dead plants and animals, and the thickening cover of fallen logs, animal carcasses, and other plant and animal remains would choke out new life.

Fortunately, decay does occur. Decomposition continually renews and enriches the earth, returning carbon, hydrogen, and nutrients to the soil, water, and air and providing the conditions needed for new life to thrive. This natural decomposition process is called *biodegradation.* "Degradation" means decay, and "bio-" refers to the fact that it is carried out by biological forces—by the huge assortment of bacteria, fungi, insects, worms, and other organisms that eat dead material and recycle it into new forms.

SCi*LINKS*
THE WORLD'S A CLICK AWAY

Topic: biodegradation
Go to: *www.sciLINKS.org*
Code: DR01

Biodegradation **refers to the biological processes that cause decay.**

Organic matter includes living and dead organisms and the wastes they produce.

Through biodegradation, dead plants and animals get broken down and so do the waste products they produce while living. For plants, these waste products include dead leaves and the remnants of seeds and blossoms. For animals, wastes include excrement and any feathers, fur, hair, antlers, shells, skin, or other parts that get shed. All of these wastes are examples of *organic matter,* material that has been created by living things.

Although all organic matter eventually will decay, some types will break down much faster than others. Depending on the type of material and the environmental conditions, decay may take place within hours or over many years. Why is biodegradation important? Not only does it clean up the mess left behind by dead bodies and other wastes, it also plays an essential role in nutrient cycling and energy flow—key processes that sustain life on Earth.

Organic compounds are chemicals that contain chains of two or more carbon atoms.

In order to live and grow, all living things need a source of energy and a source of nutrients, especially carbon. Why carbon? Life is based on carbon because this element is the basis for the sugars, proteins, starches, and other compounds that make up living things. All of these compounds consist of chains of carbon atoms linked together and combined with hydrogen, oxygen, and sometimes a few other key elements. Compounds that contain chains of two or more carbon atoms per molecule are called *organic compounds.* Organic matter is made up of organic compounds.

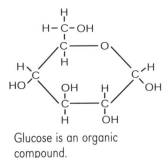

Glucose is an organic compound.

In addition to carbon and other nutrients, all living things need a source of energy to sustain life. When you need energy, you eat food. All organisms need nutrition, but they get it in a variety of ways, depending on whether they are producers or consumers.

PRODUCERS AND CONSUMERS

Green plants are called *producers* because they can make their own food. Using energy from the Sun, producers create organic matter from carbon dioxide and water. This process is called *photosynthesis*—from "photo," the Latin word for light, and "synthesis," meaning to create.

Producers use energy from the Sun to make their own food.

Through photosynthesis, green plants convert solar energy into chemical energy in the form of glucose and other simple sugars (Figure 1.1). These sugars are organic compounds, made up of carbon, hydrogen, and oxygen. Plants build them using carbon from carbon dioxide and hydrogen and oxygen from water. The leftover oxygen gets released to the atmosphere.

When plants grow, they build complex compounds such as starches and proteins by combining the simple sugars produced through photosynthesis with nutrients such as nitrogen, phosphorus, and sulfur that they take up from soil and water. Through this process, they also create *enzymes,* specialized proteins that are used to accelerate or control the rates of biochemical reactions. For example, one type of enzyme plays a crucial role in regulating the rate at which carbon dioxide is used in photosynthesis.

Animals and other organisms that cannot produce their own food are called *consumers.* Instead of absorbing carbon dioxide and converting it to

FIGURE 1.1
Through Photosynthesis, Green Plants Create
Organic Matter

Photosynthesis:

carbon dioxide + water + solar energy → organic matter + oxygen

$$6\ CO_2 \qquad 6\ H_2O \qquad\qquad\qquad C_6H_{12}O_6 \qquad 6\ O_2$$

$$\text{(glucose)}$$

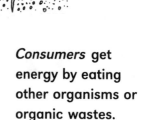

organic matter, consumers obtain their energy and nutrients by eating organic matter that has been produced by other organisms. Consumers are classified according to the kinds of food that they eat. For example, herbivores eat plants, and carnivores eat animals. Consumers that get their nutrition and energy by eating wastes are called *decomposers*. Their food consists of dead bodies, animal droppings, leaves, and all sorts of other wastes produced by living things.

Through a process that looks like the reverse of photosynthesis, both producers and consumers break down organic matter into carbon dioxide, water, and energy. This process is called *respiration*. Respiration is a confusing term because it is used in a couple of different ways. One way refers to the exchange of gases that occurs in lungs or gills as organisms breathe. But what we are referring to here is a process that takes place within each cell, including cells of plants and other organisms that don't have lungs or gills. In this process of cellular respiration, organic matter gets broken down and used as a source of energy to sustain life.

Consumers get energy by eating other organisms or organic wastes.

Decomposers get energy by eating dead organisms and wastes.

Respiration:

organic matter + oxygen → carbon dioxide + water + energy

Respiration is the process through which living things use the chemical energy that is stored in organic matter.

Many people think that plants use photosynthesis to create food and animals use respiration to break it down. This is partly correct, but it ignores the fact that respiration is carried out by all living things—green plants included. When green plants are exposed to light, they produce their own food through photosynthesis. But just like animals, plants carry out respiration constantly, throughout the day and night, to support growth, reproduction, and all of the day-to-day functions of life.

NUTRIENT CYCLES AND ENERGY FLOWS

Through the processes of photosynthesis and respiration, carbon continuously cycles through living and nonliving forms (Figure 1.2). Carbon gets incorporated into organic matter by green plants through photosynthesis. Then these organic molecules are broken down through respiration by all types of organisms—plants, animals, and microbes. Respiration provides organisms with energy, and it also releases carbon dioxide back into the atmosphere where it once again becomes available for uptake by plants.

FIGURE 1.2
Carbon Cycles between Living and Nonliving Forms

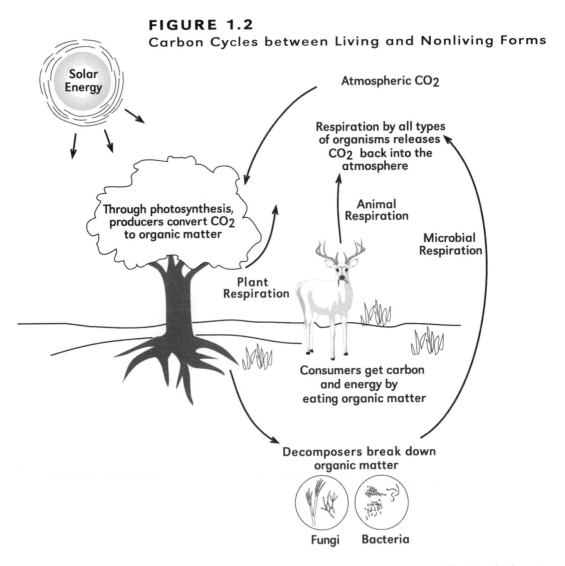

You may be familiar with diagrams of a typical food web showing who eats what in a lake or pond (Figure 1.3). The producers in this aquatic food web include single-celled algae as well as rooted and floating plants such as water lilies and duckweed. The smallest consumers are tiny organisms such as protozoa that get energy by eating algae, other tiny organisms, and particles of organic matter. Then they in turn are eaten by secondary consumers such as aquatic invertebrates, which get eaten by higher-level consumers such as fish, frogs, turtles, and birds.

FIGURE 1.3
A Typical Food Web in a Lake or Pond

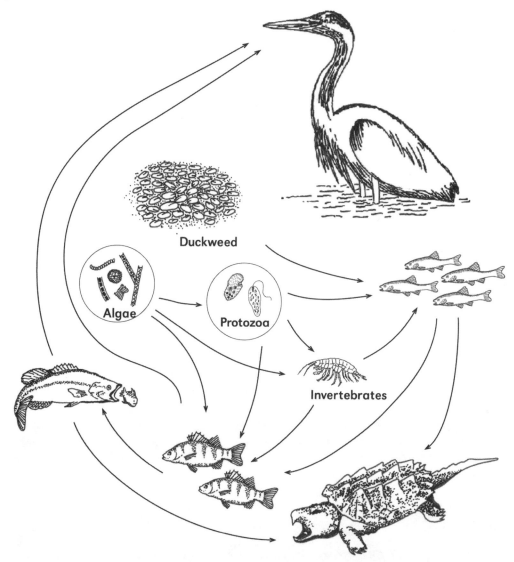

Duckweed

Algae

Protozoa

Invertebrates

At each step in a food web, organisms obtain energy from the food that they eat. However, energy does not cycle through the living and nonliving environment like carbon does. Instead, it flows in one direction, from producers to consumers at various levels of food webs. At each level, organisms use cellular respiration to release the chemical energy stored in sugars, starches, and other organic compounds. Some of this energy gets used to support life processes, but much is lost to the environment in the form of heat.

Think about how you get hot when you exercise vigorously. This heat is caused by the cellular respiration that fuels your exercise. Cellular respiration accomplishes this same sort of energy conversion in all types of organisms, from microbes to mountain lions. That's why energy flow through an ecosystem commonly is represented as a pyramid—at each step there is less chemical energy available because of the losses in the form of heat (Figure 1.4).

SCI
LINKS.
THE WORLD'S A CLICK AWAY

Topic: food webs
Go to: www.sciLINKS.org
Code: DR02

FIGURE 1.4
A Typical Energy Pyramid in a Lake or Pond

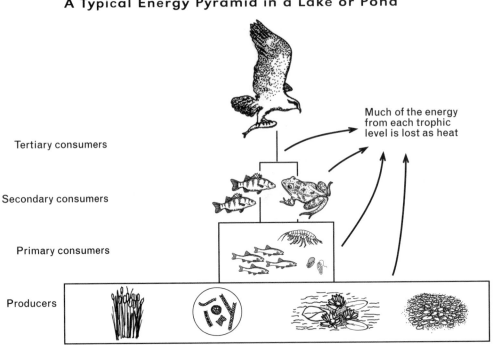

Tertiary consumers

Secondary consumers

Primary consumers

Producers

Much of the energy from each trophic level is lost as heat

Something is missing from the food web and energy pyramid represented in Figures 1.3 and 1.4. What happens to the nutrients and chemical energy contained in organisms when they die, or in the wastes that they produce while alive? Decomposers use these sources of energy and nutrients. At each level of a food web or energy pyramid, decomposers take care of the wastes that are produced. In the process of obtaining nutrition by eating organic wastes, they provide a vital link in global nutrient cycles. For example, decomposers convert carbon that is tied up in organic compounds back into carbon dioxide, making it available to once again be taken up by plants and used in photosynthesis.

Waste or Resource?

We humans may have a hard time imagining eating animal droppings, but these wastes provide valuable sources of protein and other nutrients to dung beetles and a wide range of other decomposer microorganisms.

If you were a dung beetle, your life would be devoted to finding, storing, and eating the dung of larger animals. There are thousands of species of dung beetles in the world, native to every continent except Antarctica. All of them specialize in eating animal droppings of one sort or another. To store food away from competing decomposers, these beetles carve out pieces of dung and roll them into balls. They lay their eggs inside these balls and bury them underground. When the eggs hatch, the dung provides food for the larvae as they grow and develop into adults.

Although dung beetles are an obvious type of decomposer, they have lots of company in the invertebrate world. For example, worms, millipedes, slugs, and sow bugs all are decomposers that feast on decaying organic matter.

The most important organisms in the biodegradation process are ones you cannot see—the *microscopic* organisms called microorganisms or *microbes*. Among leaves and logs on the forest floor, in a steaming pile of hay or manure, or in a compost pile, a huge assortment of these less visible decomposer organisms are at work. All decomposers use dead organic matter as a source of energy and nutrients; then they in turn may become food for a wide variety of other consumer organisms.

Decay-causing microbes are present in every type of habitat, even on living things. Have you ever wondered why an apple core will quickly rot when buried in moist soil, but a carrot growing in the same soil will not? As long as an organism is alive, its natural defenses hold back the forces of decay. But as soon as a plant or animal dies, it becomes food for a wide array of decomposers. Who are these decomposers? Most are classified as either fungi or bacteria.

Microbes include all organisms that are too small to be seen without a microscope.

Biodegradation is carried out primarily by microbes.

CLASSIFICATION OF LIVING THINGS

Ever since the 1700s, scientists have been interested in naming organisms and organizing them into broad groups called *kingdoms*. Within each kingdom, the organisms share some important characteristics and are thought to have evolved from common ancestors. At first, all living things were classified into either plant or animal kingdoms. Over the years, scientists have proposed modifications to this classification scheme based on new discoveries about living things. In 1784, for example, scientists proposed adding a third kingdom—the fungi—including mushrooms as well as a vast world of less visible organisms such as molds and yeasts.

In some ways, fungi are similar to plants. When you look at a mushroom, it certainly seems more like a plant than an animal. However, when Anton van Leeuwenhoek and other scientists first started using microscopes to study living things, they discovered that fungi have some characteristics that set them apart from the plant kingdom. For example, fungal cells do not contain chlorophyll, the chemical that enables green plants to carry out photosynthesis. Instead, fungi release specialized proteins called *enzymes* that break down organic matter into substances that get absorbed into their cells and then further digested. Once this discovery was made, scientists proposed assigning fungi to their own kingdom.

Various two- or three-kingdom classification systems were used for almost 200 years. This changed in 1969, when Dr. Robert Whittaker, an ecologist at Cornell University, proposed that life could best be organized into five kingdoms. In addition to plants, animals, and fungi, he proposed two new kingdoms:

▶ the Protista, including simple organisms such as amoebas that have a nucleus, and

▶ the Monera, including bacteria and similar single-celled organisms that don't have true nuclei.

In recent years, this five-kingdom classification scheme has once again come under scientific debate. The classification system will continue to change as new discoveries about DNA and genetics help to trace the evolutionary relationships connecting all forms of life.

The group of organisms that we call *microbes* or *microorganisms* is defined according to size rather than kingdoms. The only feature that they have in common is that they are too small to be seen without a microscope. Microorganisms include bacteria, fungi, and single-celled plants and animals—clearly representing a broad range of kingdoms. The group that we call *decomposers* also is found in more than one kingdom. Decomposers are defined by function—they are the organisms that cause biodegradation.

BIODEGRADATION ON LAND

In a soil food web, microorganisms are the most numerous living things and also play the largest role in decomposition. A single spoonful of soil can contain up to a billion bacteria and hundreds of thousands of fungi.

Fungi

Fungi are visible in the form of mushrooms, molds, and yeasts, but they also grow long microscopic threads that stretch throughout soil and decaying vegetation such as rotting logs. Fungi serve a vital role in biodegradation of plants. Plant cell walls contain cellulose, a complex compound that cannot be digested by most animals. Lignin, another hard-to-degrade compound, forms long chains that link cells together in wood, straw, and other plant stems. Fungi provide the first line of attack in breaking down these tough compounds, turning them into forms that are usable by bacteria and other organisms.

A few types of fungi are predators, specialized to capture and digest nematodes, tiny roundworms that are described below. These fungi create sticky nets or noose-like loops to trap their prey. Then thread-like filaments from the fungi extend into the captured nematodes and digest them as a source of energy and nitrogen.

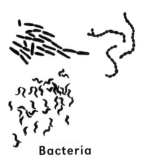

Bacteria

Bacteria are microscopic, single-celled organisms shaped like rods, spheres, or spirals. They are among the most abundant organisms on earth. Most bacteria are decomposers, although some species are able to create their own food through photosynthesis. Before bacteria can digest chemical compounds, they need to absorb the compounds into their cells. Many compounds are too large to be absorbed directly, so microbes release enzymes to pre-digest these substances into smaller pieces that can be absorbed and used as food.

Protozoa

If you drain water from a sample of moist soil or compost and observe it under a microscope, you are likely to see tiny, single-celled organisms called protozoa. Members of the Protista kingdom, protozoa such as amoebas live in the thin films of water surrounding soil particles. They feed on bacteria, fungi, other protozoa, and dissolved organic matter. Because they digest organic matter and then get eaten by higher organisms, protozoa can provide important links in decomposer food chains.

Nematode

Nematodes are another type of tiny organism you are likely to find in water drained from soil or compost. Nematodes are nonsegmented worms, about the width of a human hair. They are extremely abundant and diverse. Some species eat decaying vegetation, some eat bacteria or fungi, and others prey on protozoa or other nematodes.

Larger organisms also help to break down organic matter in soil. If you sift through the layer of leaves and other decaying vegetation at the soil surface, you are likely to find an assortment of invertebrates such as millipedes, sow bugs, snails, slugs, and earthworms. These organisms shred decaying vegetation, breaking it down both physically and chemically. The **Soil Invertebrate Identification Sheet** (p. 38) describes common invertebrates found in soil and compost.

Sow Bug

Together all of these organisms make up complex decomposer food webs (Figure 1.5). Organisms such as slugs and sow bugs eat dead plants and animals. Others such as dung beetles prefer wastes that have already passed through the guts of other organisms. Microbes play a central role in decomposer food webs. As they digest wastes to meet their own nutritional needs, microbes also convert the organic matter into chemical forms that are more usable by a wide range of invertebrates. When worms eat decaying vegetation, they get their nutrition primarily by digesting the microbes growing on the organic matter rather than from the vegetation itself. Decomposer food webs also include predators such as centipedes that use poison glands in their jaws to paralyze prey such as small worms, insect larvae, insects, and spiders.

Centipede

FIGURE 1.5
Food Web among Soil Organisms

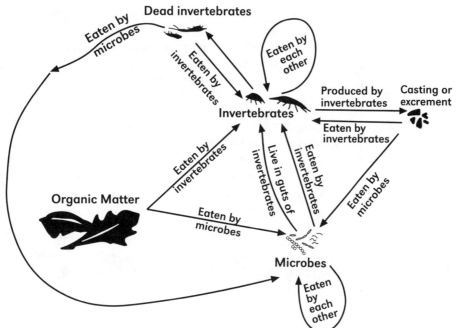

In soil, the end product of decomposition is humus, a stable mixture of complex compounds. Humus does continue to biodegrade, but the process occurs slowly over a period of years because the easier-to-degrade compounds have already been broken down. Topsoil consists mostly of humus. You may have seen it for sale at garden centers—it is valuable for plant growth because it acts like a sponge, helping to hold water and nutrients in the upper soil layers where they remain available for uptake by plants.

BIODEGRADATION IN WATER

Biodegradation takes place in every type of habitat, even in the purest mountain streams. If you flip over rocks in a swift mountain stream, you are likely to find mayfly nymphs and other aquatic invertebrates scurrying for cover. What do these organisms find to eat? The rocks may be coated with a layer of algae, but other plants are likely to be scarce because of the low nutrient concentrations. Instead, stream organisms rely on input of organic wastes from surrounding land. Leaves, twigs, and other organic materials fall into the water or are washed in by runoff or snowmelt. These materials form the base for the food web in streams.

Mayfly Nymph

Many of the invertebrates that live in mountain streams are scavengers, adapted to eating organic debris left behind by other animals and plants. Some of these invertebrates gradually shred the leaves that enter the stream from the surrounding land. Others catch particles from the current as the water flows by. Still others feed by scraping bacteria and algae off the surfaces of rocks. Finally, all of these types of invertebrates become food for trout and other higher-level consumers in aquatic food webs.

The same forces of decomposition that take place in flowing water also occur in ponds and lakes. Each year, plants and animals grow and then die and decompose, continuing the cycling of nutrients through the ecosystem.

Organic Pollution

Through the work of decomposer organisms, organic matter in lakes and streams gets broken down and used to support new life. This sounds useful to humans—why not just dump our organic wastes into the water and let natural biodegradation processes take care of them? Although this sounds like a reasonable idea, there is a limit to the biodegradation capacity of natural waterways.

If too much manure or untreated sewage enters a stream, drastic changes in stream life will occur. Populations of decomposer bacteria will grow rapidly because of the increased food supply. As bacteria work to break down the organic wastes, they use up oxygen and produce carbon dioxide. As a result, dissolved oxygen levels may drop so low that sensitive species of fish such as salmon and trout will be wiped out.

Aquatic invertebrates also are affected by dissolved oxygen. Stonefly nymphs and beetle larvae called "water pennies" are examples of stream invertebrates that cannot live in streams that have become polluted with too much organic matter. These organisms cling to rocks in streams where the rapidly flowing currents normally carry high levels of dissolved oxygen. When oxygen levels drop too low, sensitive invertebrates such as these will not be able to survive.

Gradually, a few types of organisms that are adapted to life under low-oxygen conditions will begin to move into stream sections that are polluted with too much organic matter. For example, sludge worms are adapted to living with very little dissolved oxygen, and they commonly are found in water with organic pollution. These worms live with their heads buried in muddy sediments and their bodies waving through the water to capture as much oxygen as possible. Because few types of organisms are adapted to life in polluted waters, the diversity of organisms tends to be much lower there than in areas with higher oxygen concentrations.

As sewage-polluted water flows downstream, natural purification gradually occurs. Although the stream remains highly impacted at the pollution source, this impact diminishes with distance downstream. This occurs because the organic matter gradually breaks down and dissolved oxygen levels gradually return to normal. The section of the stream in which this occurs is called the *zone of recovery* (Figure 1.6). The length of this zone depends on the size of the river or stream and the amount of organic pollution it receives. A small stream with a large input of organic pollution can be impacted for many miles downstream of the pollution source.

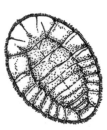

Water Penny (top view)

Water Penny (side view)

Sludge Worm

In the *zone of recovery,* natural biodegradation processes gradually clean up the organic pollution in a stream.

FIGURE 1.6
Stream Life Gradually Recovers as Organic Matter Biodegrades Downstream of a Pollution Source

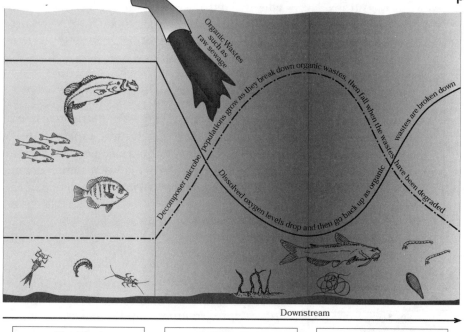

Downstream

Clean Zone	Pollution Zone	Zone of Recovery
Inhabited by highly sensitive organisms such as mayfly, stonefly and caddisfly nymphs, and trout, perch, and bass.	Life is limited to highly tolerant organisms such as sludge worms, leeches, and catfish.	Sensitive organisms become more common with distance downstream as biodegradation occurs.

Eutrophication

A slightly different form of organic pollution occurs when excess vegetation grows in lakes, rivers, or coastal waters. Rather than input of organic matter such as manure or untreated sewage, in this case the problem is caused by input of too much fertilizer. The fertilizer causes algae and other aquatic plants to grow out of balance with the natural forces of decay and renewal. This over-fertilization process is called *eutrophication,* derived from Greek words meaning "well fed."

Fertilizers commonly contain three essential plant nutrients: nitrogen, phosphorus, and potassium. Just as these nutrients increase the growth of crops, lawns, golf courses, and gardens, they also stimulate growth of algae and other aquatic vegetation. When water bodies receive nutrient-rich run-off from fertilized land, they may become eutrophic.

In fresh water, plant growth usually is limited by the amount of available phosphorus. In oceans and estuaries, nitrogen is more likely to be the nutrient in shortest supply. When extra nutrients are provided, they trigger faster growth of algae and other aquatic plants. Within certain limits, increased growth causes no harm. But if nutrient levels become too high, lakes, rivers, or coastal waters will become choked with mats of algae or beds of rooted vegetation.

When *eutrophication* occurs, high rates of biodegradation use up dissolved oxygen in aquatic systems.

SCi LINKS
THE WORLD'S A CLICK AWAY

Topic: eutrophication
Go to: *www.sciLINKS.org*
Code: DR03

Aquatic plants add oxygen to the water through photosynthesis, so you might think that the more they grow, the better. However, plants and animals also use oxygen through respiration. As a result, dissolved oxygen levels in eutrophic waters tend to fluctuate widely, with high levels during the day but low levels at night. Another problem is that photosynthesis occurs only in the surface layers where plants have access to sunlight. When the mats of algae and other plants and animals die, they sink. Oxygen gets used up in the deeper waters as all of this organic matter decomposes. As a result, the fish and other organisms that live in cool, deep waters may no longer be able to survive.

Over a period of hundreds or thousands of years, water bodies may naturally become more eutrophic due to natural inputs of nutrient-rich sediments. Human-caused eutrophication occurs much more rapidly, causing ecological problems by throwing off the natural balance between rates of growth and decay. In the worst cases, this results in masses of rotting organic matter, and habitats that no longer can support sensitive species of fish and other aquatic life.

CONCLUSION

Biodegradation is a natural process that is essential to the continuation of energy flow and nutrient cycling in ecosystems. Energy is neither created nor destroyed, but we think of it as flowing rather than cycling through ecosystems because life on Earth requires continual input of energy from the Sun. Photosynthetic organisms convert solar energy to chemical energy, which is used by the producers themselves and by all types of consumers and decomposers. Without continued input of solar energy, life as we know it would end because at each level of every food web much of the chemical energy gets lost in the form of heat. Energy flow through an ecosystem is represented as a pyramid because of these losses in chemical energy at each level.

Unlike energy, the Earth does not receive new inputs of nutrients such as carbon. Instead, carbon and other nutrients constantly cycle between living and nonliving forms. For example, organisms incorporate carbon into organic compounds such as sugars, carbohydrates, and proteins. Through cellular respiration by all types of organisms, these organic compounds get broken down and carbon dioxide is released back into the environment.

On land and in water, decomposers work to break down plant and animal debris, releasing nutrients needed for new growth. These continuous cycles of growth and decomposition form the basis for all life on Earth. However, it is possible to overwhelm the natural forces of decay and renewal. For example, if too much manure, sewage, or other organic matter is dumped into a stream, dissolved oxygen concentrations drop too low to support sensitive forms of aquatic life. Over-fertilization causes similar problems in nutrient-rich waterways that become eutrophic when excessive growth of aquatic plants creates more organic matter than the system can decompose without ecological harm.

The following chapters focus on ways in which people use natural forces of biodegradation to clean up wastes and prevent pollution problems such as these.

DISCUSSION QUESTIONS

▶ Could we live without microbes? How do they affect the environment?

▶ Why do we say that nutrients "cycle" but that energy "flows" in ecosystems? What roles do decomposers play in these processes?

▶ If matter can be neither created nor destroyed, where does it go when plants or animals decompose?

CHAPTER 2

HARNESSING NATURAL DECAY

HUMAN WASTE DISPOSAL PROCESSES

In the early days of human settlements, people buried their wastes or simply tossed them out the window. Imagine the filth and odors in cities during the mid-1800s, when the streets were full of trash, human sewage, animal droppings, and even the bodies of dead horses. Pigs ran wild, eating wastes but also leaving behind their own droppings. In New York City, the air was described as smelling like "bad eggs dissolved in ammonia."[1]

Not only were the odors intense, the wastes also attracted rats, roaches, and other disease-carrying animals and insects. Epidemics of cholera and other diseases were common. In 1903, Cornell University was faced with a typhoid epidemic. The infirmary was overflowing with typhoid patients, and 82 people died during the worst three-month period. Cornell students demanded that the university provide a temporary supply of pure water, and the university president responded by asking all students to leave town because their lives were at risk. The cause of the disease was unknown, but water contamination was suspected. Finally, a sanitation expert from New York City brought the epidemic under control. Residents were warned to boil their drinking water, and cleanup efforts focused on removing the numerous outhouses hanging directly over stream banks.

By 1910, public health concerns had led most American cities to adopt methods for public collection and disposal of both trash and sewage. The streets became cleaner, but the wastes still were not treated in the ways we take for granted today. As recently as 1965, garbage and raw sewage routinely were dumped into U.S. waterways. In many coastal cities, garbage and sewage sludge were loaded on barges and dumped in the ocean.

Over the years both the volume and content of garbage and sewage began to cause problems in rivers, lakes, and oceans. Large numbers of dead fish washing up on shorelines indicated that the natural forces of biodegradation can easily become overloaded. Gradually people began to realize that dumping garbage and sewage into waterways was causing pollution and killing fish and wildlife.

---

[1]Bettmann, O. L. 1974. *The Good Old Days—They Were Terrible!* New York: Random House, p. 7.

Another form of pollution was plastic litter, washed up onto beaches by waves and currents. In the industrial age following World War II, a huge assortment of new products was developed. Many items were designed to be used only once, then thrown away. For the first time, many of these products were made of plastics and other synthetic chemical compounds. As a result, human wastes began to contain many more articles that do not biodegrade.

BIODEGRADABLE PLASTICS

Cellophane was one of the first packaging materials created by scientists. Made from wood pulp, it was widely used for food packaging until the 1930s, when it was largely replaced with other plastic materials that do not rip so easily but also do not biodegrade.

Because of growing concern about plastic litter in oceans and along highways, in the 1970s biodegradable packaging materials once again became a popular idea. At first, these bags and food packages were made of conventional plastics such as polystyrene, held together by biodegradable starches. The problem with these mixtures is that they are not fully biodegradable. When the starch decays, the bag or other item breaks down into smaller pieces, but the polystyrene pieces remain quite resistant to decay.

More recently, inventors have developed plastics that are fully biodegradable because they are made entirely of substances such as potato starch or cornstarch. In one example, scientists were experimenting with ways of keeping breakfast cereal crunchy in milk when they stumbled across a way of making biodegradable packaging "peanuts." Unlike polystyrene, these pieces, made from cornstarch, dissolve in water and rapidly break down into carbon dioxide and water when composted or exposed to the environment.

LANDFILLS

In 2000, Americans produced more than 230 million tons of municipal solid waste, an average of 4.5 pounds per person per day. Fifty-five percent of this was sent to landfills (Figure 1.7).

FIGURE 1.7
Fate of America's Garbage in 2000

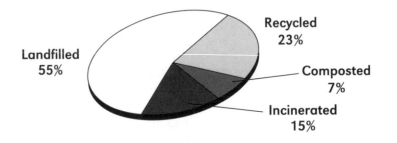

Source: Environmental Protection Agency, Office of Solid Waste and Emergency Response. 2002. *Municipal Solid Waste in the United States: 2000 Facts and Figures.* EPA530-R-02-001. Available online at *http://www.epa.gov.*

Of the wastes sent to landfills, typically about 70% consists of biodegradable wastes such as paper products, yard wastes, and food. The remaining 30% represents wastes made of metals, glass, plastics, and other materials that are resistant to decay. You might think that biodegradable wastes would break down quickly in landfills. However, Dr. William Rathje, an archaeologist at the University of Arizona, discovered the decay rate to be surprisingly slow.

Instead of excavating the remains of ancient civilizations, Dr. Rathje has focused his archaeological research on modern garbage. Digging through landfills in cities ranging from Toronto to Tucson, he and his teams have found 40-year-old newspapers that they could still read and food that showed few signs of decay.

Why have these organic materials not broken down? The answer lies in the nutritional and environmental needs of decomposer microbes compared with the conditions that exist in a typical landfill environment. Because of the low levels of available oxygen and moisture, biodegradable items do not decay as quickly as you might expect.

Modern sanitary landfills are designed to contain wastes in a way that protects public health and environmental quality. This means covering the garbage each day with a layer of soil, compost, or other materials to prevent odors or problems with rodents, flies, and other pests. It also means keeping the wastes as dry as possible to prevent runoff and leaching of contaminants. When new landfills are built in the United States, the bottoms are lined with dense clay and plastic liners to prevent drainage of hazardous chemicals into surrounding soil and groundwater. Once landfills become full, the surface gets capped with a layer of clay to keep precipitation out. This cap also limits airflow through the buried garbage.

Because of the low oxygen levels, the decomposer microbes that live in landfills represent species that are able to combine carbon with hydrogen instead of oxygen during the process of respiration. Rather than carbon dioxide (CO_2), these microbes produce methane (CH_4), an explosive gas that commonly is vented from landfills or collected for energy (methane is the main ingredient in natural gas, a common fuel for heating systems).

In recent years, people have begun experimenting with the idea of managing landfills to provide conditions that promote rapid biodegradation but also protect the environment from air and water pollution. In these systems, called *bioreactor landfills*, the moisture levels, airflow, and temperatures are managed to promote rapid decay of organic materials such as food wastes, paper, grass clippings, and other plant materials. Organic wastes such as these currently represent over half the material sent to landfills (Figure 1.8).

SCI
LINKS.
THE WORLD'S A CLICK AWAY

Topic: landfills
Go to: www.sciLINKS.org
Code: DR04

FIGURE 1.8
Typical Composition of Wastes Sent to U.S. Landfills

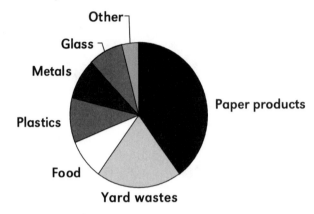

Source: Environmental Protection Agency, Office of Solid Waste and Emergency Response. 2002. *Municipal Solid Waste in the United States: 2000 Facts and Figures.* EPA530-R-02-001. Available online at *http://www.epa.gov.*

There are two types of bioreactor landfills, designed for different purposes. One type is designed to produce methane, a useful source of energy. Because methane is produced by microbes that grow when little or no oxygen is available, these sites are operated under low-oxygen conditions. The reverse is true for the second type of bioreactor landfill, in which the goal is to maximize the rate of biodegradation rather than the rate of methane production. Biodegradation proceeds more quickly when oxygen is available because the types of microbe that grow using oxygen are more efficient degraders than the ones that can survive in low-oxygen environments.

The conditions that are desirable at this second type of bioreactor landfill are the same ones that are important in making compost: sufficient moisture, aeration, and the right mix of materials to promote rapid growth of oxygen-loving decomposer microbes.

COMPOSTING

Of the 232 million tons of garbage produced by Americans in 2000, 30% was recycled or composted rather than sent to landfills or incinerators (Figure 1.7). Composting is defined as the process of decomposing organic materials under controlled conditions. You may find it easier to think of composting as a form of recycling, in which organic wastes such as food scraps and yard clippings are recycled into a resource that can be used to enrich the soil and support plant growth.

Composting involves providing conditions that cause organic materials to decompose more quickly than they would without management. Think about leaves and logs lying on the ground in a forest. The leaves will break down and disappear within a year. Logs will take much longer, but they too eventually will crumble away. Composting accelerates these natural processes of decay by providing optimal conditions for growth of decomposer organisms.

Given the right proportions of moisture, air, and nutrients to support rapid growth of microbes, compost will become hot. For example, the temperature in the middle of an outdoor compost pile may rise to 55°C within the first few days of mixing the organic materials, even when surrounding air temperatures are below freezing. This happens because microbes produce heat through cellular respiration as they work to digest the organic matter.

Compost Biology

Together, many different species of bacteria, fungi, and invertebrates interact to break down organic matter and produce compost. The same types of organisms that play important roles in biodegradation in nature (see Chapter 1) also are key players in the composting process. These organisms get food energy by eating dead leaves and other organic materials. Through digestion, they degrade large organic compounds such as sugars, starches, and proteins into simpler compounds, including carbon dioxide and water.

The most visible compost organisms are invertebrates such as worms, millipedes, and sow bugs, but microscopic bacteria and fungi accomplish most of the biodegradation. When a worm eats its way through a rotten apple, research has shown that the worm obtains more of its nutrition by digesting the millions of decomposer microbes than from the apple itself.

Bacteria are responsible for most of the decomposition and heat generation in compost. They are the most nutritionally diverse group of compost organisms, using a broad range of enzymes to chemically break down a variety of organic materials.

Actinomycetes, a type of bacteria that grows long, thin filaments, helps to create the characteristic earthy smell of soil and compost. The thread-like filaments stretch through compost and break down resistant compounds such as the cellulose in leaves and wood. They are most commonly seen toward the end of the composting process, in the outer edges of the pile. Sometimes they appear as circular colonies that gradually expand in diameter.

Fungi such as molds, yeasts, and mushrooms are important in composting because they break down tough debris such as wood, straw, and other materials that are too dry, acidic, or low in nitrogen to be a useful food source for bacteria. Most fungi release digestive enzymes in order to break complex organic compounds into simpler forms that they can absorb into their cells. In the process, fungi also convert the complex compounds into forms that are digestible by bacteria and other organisms.

When compost heats up, most species of fungi can survive only in the outer layers where temperatures remain cooler. Compost molds may appear as gray or white fuzzy colonies, but many are microscopic. When you see mushrooms growing on compost, you may not realize that each is connected to an extensive network of thread-like filaments that reach through the organic matter and aid in its decomposition.

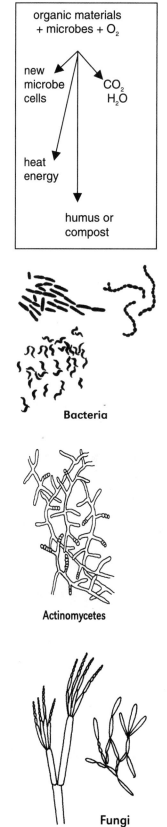

organic materials + microbes + O_2

new microbe cells

CO_2 H_2O

heat energy

humus or compost

Bacteria

Actinomycetes

Fungi

Compost Chemistry and Physics

Composting may appear to be a biological process, but chemistry and physics also play important roles. Compost microbes need carbon for energy, nitrogen to build proteins, oxygen for respiration, and moisture to support life. Given the right set of chemical and physical conditions, rapid growth and metabolism by decomposer microbes will cause the compost to heat up. This is desirable because biodegradation occurs faster at warmer temperatures (up to a limit of about 65°C).

One of the requirements for rapid growth of microbes is moisture. As an example, think about cornflakes. In the box, cornflakes and other breakfast cereals will last indefinitely because they are too dry to support growth of bacteria or fungi. However, if you leave a bowl of wet cereal sitting around, it won't be long before you notice signs of decomposition. Similarly, moisture plays a critical role in compost. If the mixture becomes too dry, decomposition will slow down because microbes will not be able to grow and reproduce.

Aeration is another important factor in composting. As organic wastes get broken down, oxygen is used up through cellular respiration by decomposer microbes. Mixing, turning, or blowing air through compost systems helps to replenish the oxygen supplies. Although organic wastes will decay either with or without oxygen, the microbes that are adapted to living in oxygen-rich environments are more efficient degraders than those that can live without oxygen.

The microbes in compost need nitrogen, carbon, oxygen, and moisture to sustain growth.

The final factor that is important to consider in composting is the nutrient content of the wastes, particularly the relative amounts of carbon and nitrogen. The ideal carbon-to-nitrogen (C:N) ratio for composting is considered to be around 30:1, meaning 30 parts carbon for each part nitrogen by weight. Why 30:1? Although the typical microbial cell is made up of carbon and nitrogen in ratios as low as 6:1, additional carbon is needed to provide the energy for metabolism and growth of new cells.

If you were a professional compost system manager, you would be likely to measure the C:N ratios and moisture contents of your compost ingredients. This would help you to ensure that the composting proceeds rapidly and achieves temperatures high enough to kill germs and weed seeds. For more casual composting, simple guidelines can take the place of measuring and calculating the optimal mix of ingredients.

Colorful wastes such as fresh grass clippings and fruit or vegetable scraps tend to be relatively high in nitrogen and moisture but low in carbon. If you tried to compost these wastes alone, you would be likely to end up with a stinky mess. Brown wastes such as wood chips, straw, autumn leaves, and shredded cardboard are the opposite—relatively low in nitrogen and moisture but high in carbon. If composted alone, these wastes would eventually biodegrade, but it would take a long time.

To achieve optimal nutrient and moisture conditions, the general rule is to mix roughly equal amounts of colorful, moist wastes with brown, dry materials. This type of mixture tends to provide the right proportion of carbon, nitrogen, and moisture to achieve heat-producing compost. Protocol 12b gives further guidelines about specific compost ingredients.

Is your compost heating up? How hot does it get? How long does it remain at peak temperatures? Because heat is generated through growth and respiration of decomposer microbes, you can use periodic temperature readings to gauge how well your compost system is working and how far the decomposition has progressed. As the available food materials get used up, microbial activity will slow down and the temperature will begin to drop. Turning or mixing the pile at this point may create another temperature peak because the relatively undecomposed wastes from the edges get mixed in, providing additional food for the decomposer microbes.

Figure 1.9 shows a typical temperature curve for a heat-producing compost system. The peak temperatures, and the length of time the compost remains hot, will depend on many factors including the size of the system, the moisture levels, and the compost ingredients. Monitoring compost temperature is a good way to see the effects of management actions such as turning the pile or adding extra water part way through the process.

FIGURE 1.9
A Typical Temperature Curve for a Heat-Producing Compost System

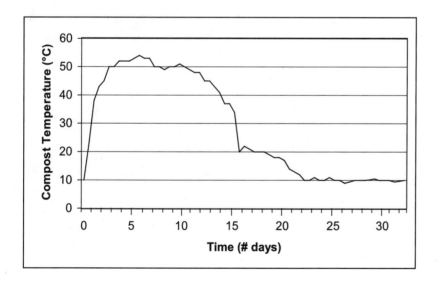

Not all composting takes place at high temperatures. A pile of autumn leaves will eventually decompose without getting hot, but it will take much longer than in a heat-producing compost system. In the leaf pile, the nitrogen and moisture levels will be too low to promote rapid growth of microbes, but these organisms will continue to grow and carry out decomposition at a slow pace until the leaves are fully degraded.

WASTEWATER TREATMENT

Composting accelerates natural forces of biodegradation on land, and wastewater treatment achieves this same goal in water. The purification systems in natural water bodies can easily be overloaded with input of too much organic waste (see Chapter 1). Wastewater treatment aims to prevent this type of pollution by degrading much of the organic matter before the water gets released into the environment.

Wastewater treatment is a broad term that includes many types of wastes and treatment processes. Here we will focus on treatment of human sewage, which is designed to accomplish two major goals: (1) removing enough organic matter to avoid ecological problems when the treated sewage gets released into natural water bodies and (2) disinfecting the sewage to kill disease-causing germs.

Wastewater treatment uses microbes to break down organic matter.

FIGURE 1.10
Diagram of a Typical Sewage Treatment System

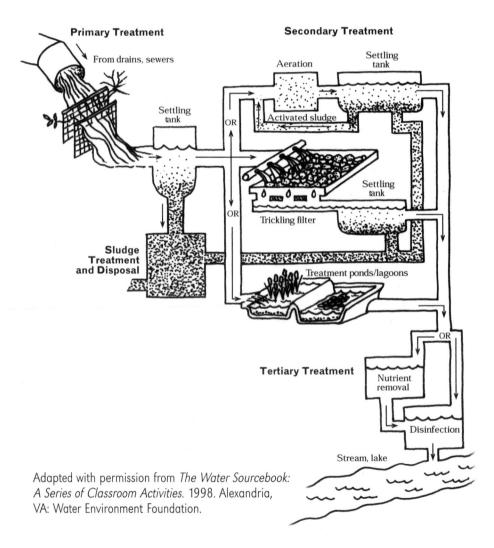

Adapted with permission from *The Water Sourcebook: A Series of Classroom Activities.* 1998. Alexandria, VA: Water Environment Foundation.

Untreated sewage contains large amounts of organic matter, including large chunks, smaller particles, and dissolved organic compounds. Bacteria and aquatic organisms use oxygen as they break down any of these sources of organic matter. If too much untreated sewage or other organic matter is added to a lake or stream, dissolved oxygen levels will drop too low to support sensitive species of fish and other aquatic life. Wastewater treatment systems are designed to remove or digest much of the organic matter so that this will not occur.

The first step in wastewater treatment is to physically remove large solids using a series of grates, screens, and settling tanks (Figure 1.10). Through this primary treatment step, about 60% of the solids in sewage get removed.

Many wastewater treatment plants also provide secondary treatment. This is the stage at which most biodegradation takes place. Using the same types of natural biodegradation processes that occur in streams and lakes, secondary treatment systems use microbes to decompose organic matter before sewage gets released into the environment.

Secondary treatment occurs in a variety of ways, all of which promote growth of bacteria and other microbes that eat organic wastes. In some treatment systems, wastewater sits in a large tank or series of tanks with air bubbling through to keep the oxygen levels high. In the "activated sludge" process, some of the solids that settle out during treatment get added back into these aeration tanks. Because these solids provide a rich source of microbes specialized in breaking down organic wastes, circulating them back into the treatment process speeds up the rate at which biodegradation occurs.

In some treatment plants, sewage is sent through a series of trickling filters. These are beds of stones or other large particles coated with slimy layers called *biofilms.* The biofilms consist of complex communities of microorganisms that eat organic wastes. As wastewater trickles past, microbes digest dissolved organic matter and break it down into simpler chemical forms. After flowing through the trickling filter, the treated wastewater gets passed through settling tanks to remove solids that occasionally break loose from the biofilms. As a finishing touch, the water may also get filtered through beds of sand to remove fine particles. Sometimes chemicals such as alum are added to cause tiny particles to clump together so that they will settle out or can more readily be filtered out of solution.

To test the success of primary and secondary treatment, scientists perform a test called biochemical oxygen demand (BOD). This measures the amount of dissolved oxygen that gets consumed in a sample over a five-day incubation period. Each wastewater treatment plant has a discharge permit that specifies the allowable BOD level for treated wastewater, which depends on site-specific conditions such as the size and condition of the receiving water body. Generally this ranges between 8 and 150 mg/L BOD, compared with up to 300 mg/L for sewage that has not yet been treated.

In most cases, wastewater treatment stops at the secondary level. However, if the water body that will be receiving the wastewater needs to be pro-

Primary treatment uses physical processes to remove large solids from wastewater.

Secondary treatment depends on biodegradation.

SCI LINKS.
THE WORLD'S A CLICK AWAY
Topic: wastewater treatment
Go to: www.sciLINKS.org
Code: DR05

SCI LINKS.
THE WORLD'S A CLICK AWAY
Topic: biofilm
Go to: www.sciLINKS.org
Code: DR06

In *tertiary treatment,* nutrients are removed through biological or chemical processes.

tected from nutrient additions, a third level of treatment may be added. The goal of tertiary treatment is to lower the concentrations of dissolved nutrients, primarily phosphorus and nitrogen, before the wastewater is released into the environment. One approach is to add chemicals that combine with nutrients to form solid particles that precipitate out of solution. Another approach is to grow water hyacinths, duckweed, or other aquatic plants in the treated wastewater. As these plants grow, they take up dissolved nutrients. Harvesting the plants removes nutrients from the system so they will not be released back into solution when the plants die and decompose.

Whether sewage goes through tertiary, secondary, or only primary levels of treatment, the final step in all cases is disinfection to kill disease-causing organisms. This most commonly is accomplished by adding chlorine, just like in swimming pools where chlorine is used to kill germs. Chlorine can kill larger organisms too, and you may have heard news reports of fish kills caused by chlorinated wastewater. Under normal conditions, dilution rapidly reduces chlorine concentrations when wastewater enters a lake, river, or stream. But if water levels are lower than usual, or chlorine levels are unusually high, fish kills can occur. Many states therefore require removal of excess chlorine before discharge of treated wastewater into the environment.

Additional treatment is required for sludges, the solids removed during wastewater treatment, in order to reduce their odor and water content before disposal. Depending on the disposal method, sludges also may undergo treatment to further decompose the organic matter or to kill disease-causing organisms.

The most common method of sludge processing is to hold it in a large tank under anaerobic (no-oxygen) conditions. Microbes that are adapted to life without oxygen digest the sludge and produce methane and other gases that can be burned to produce electricity. Other sludge processing techniques include incineration or chemical stabilization, followed by disposal in a landfill. Sludge also can be composted by mixing it with wood chips or other dry, high-carbon materials.

Some treated sludges meet criteria specified by the federal and state governments for specific uses such as spreading on agricultural fields or in home gardens. Land spreading is controversial because sludges contain more than just nutrients such as nitrogen and phosphorus. For example, they may also contain disease-causing germs as well as residues of pesticides, solvents, and various other chemicals that get sent down the drains in contributing households, businesses, and industries.

Common sludge contaminants such as lead and cadmium can be harmful to human health, so deciding what concentration is acceptable to spread on farmland or in gardens is not a simple matter. Setting standards for acceptable concentrations of contaminants is highly controversial because it depends not only on scientific data but also on decisions about what levels of risk are acceptable to individuals and to society as a whole. (For more information on sludge, go to *http://www.cfe.cornell.edu/wmi/sludge.html.* See *As-*

sessing Toxic Risk [2001], the first book in the Cornell Scientific Inquiry Series, for more information about chemical risk.)

Using Wetlands to Purify Wastewater

Wetlands form a natural water treatment system. As water trickles through a wetland, solid particles settle out, and microbes break down dissolved and solid organic matter. As the plants grow, they take up dissolved nutrients. Wetland plants and sediments also help to break down some types of pesticides, petroleum products, and other contaminants.

In thousands of European towns and a growing number of U.S. locations, humans are taking advantage of wetland treatment processes by building artificial wetlands for wastewater treatment. In some cases, the entire treatment process occurs as wastewater trickles through artificial marshes and ponds. More commonly, wetland plants are used in the final stages of wastewater treatment to remove nutrients and heavy metals such as mercury, cadmium, and lead. Wetland plants that accumulate heavy metals such as these can then be harvested and disposed of in an incinerator or landfill.

If the concentration of heavy metals and other contaminants in the wastewater is low, then wetland plants serve primarily to remove excess nutrients. When these plants are harvested, they may be able to be used as fertilizer on farm fields and pastures. This is the case in Devils Lake, North Dakota, where the town's wastewater gets treated as it flows through a series of wetlands. First, solids are removed in settling ponds and lagoons. Then the sewage trickles through a cattail marsh, where microbes break down organic matter, and plants and animals absorb nutrients. Finally, the wastewater enters large ponds, where millions of tiny floating duckweed plants remove nutrients and further purify the water. Using an aquatic tractor, hundreds of tons of duckweed are harvested each year and used to fertilize farm fields and pastures.

Similarly, the town of Arcata, California, uses wetlands to treat its sewage. Here, the wastewater spends about 50 days traveling through a series of ponds and marshes before being released into the ocean. In addition to purifying Arcata's wastewater, the wetlands serve as an attractive city park and bird sanctuary.

DISCUSSION QUESTIONS

▸ Biodegradable plastics sometimes are mentioned as a useful way to slow the rate at which landfills are filling up. Would you say that they are a good solution to the landfill crisis? Why or why not?

▸ What do you think determines how many and what types of microbes will be present in a sample of compost?

▸ Do you think the microbes in compost are the same or different species from the ones in wastewater? Why?

CHAPTER 3

BIOREMEDIATION:
USING MICROBES TO CLEAN UP CONTAMINATED SITES

What would you do if you needed to clean up many tons of soil and sediments that are heavily contaminated with explosives such as TNT? The U.S. Army has faced this situation at military sites around the country. One way of cleaning up these contaminated soils is to burn them in incinerators. However, incineration tends to be expensive because of the energy costs involved in trucking large quantities of soil to an incinerator and then fueling the fire to make it burn. The Army decided to try composting instead, hoping that this might provide a less expensive and more environmentally friendly method of cleaning up the contaminated soils.

When you think of composting, you probably don't think of adding substances such as TNT, oil, or other toxic or hazardous compounds to the compost mix. However, the same biodegradation processes that work to break down food scraps and other organic materials can also be put to work degrading some types of pollutants.

This is an example of a process called *bioremediation*. "Remediate" means to solve a problem. As you can probably guess, "bioremediate" means to use biological organisms to solve an environmental problem. In nature, bacteria, fungi, and other microorganisms are constantly at work breaking down organic matter. Some of these decomposers can use pollutants that contain organic compounds as a source of food. Although compounds such as TNT are poisonous to humans, to the right type of microbes, these chemicals are a useful source of nutrition. Bioremediation accelerates the natural breakdown process by providing fertilizer, oxygen, or whatever environmental conditions are necessary for rapid growth of the pollution-eating organisms.

SCI LINKS
THE WORLD'S A CLICK AWAY

Topic: bioremediation
Go to: *www.sciLINKS.org*
Code: DR07

Bioremediation uses bacteria and other microorganisms to clean up pollution.

FIGURE 1.11
Composting Is Used for Bioremediation of Some Types
of Contaminants

Photo by Jean Bonhotal, Cornell Waste Management Institute

**Composting of
contaminated soils is
one form of
bioremediation.**

Composting is one form of bioremediation (Figure 1.11), and it is proving effective at cleaning up the Army's TNT-contaminated soils. TNT is a complex compound made up of carbon, nitrogen, oxygen, and hydrogen. When combined with more conventional compost ingredients such as manure, sawdust, straw, and food scraps, this explosive compound gets broken down into harmless chemical forms. The Army has found that it can save both money and fuel by composting rather than incinerating the contaminated sediments.

Oil drilling sites provide another example of bioremediation through composting. The oily sludge at these sites can be combined with straw or wood chips, then composted. With enough moisture, air, and nitrogen, the mixture will heat up as microbes convert the wastes to compost. In nature, the oily wastes would slowly break down over a period of years or even decades. Composting accelerates this process to just a few months and produces a rich soil-like mixture that can be used in restoring the land that was torn up during the drilling process.

DEGRADING GROUNDWATER CONTAMINANTS

One of the most common groundwater pollutants in the United States is gasoline, which seeps into the ground from leaky storage tanks and pipelines. Although biodegradation does occur in groundwater, it tends to take place extremely slowly because of the cold temperatures and low oxygen levels. Bioremediation accelerates the natural water treatment processes by providing oxygen and whatever additional nutrients are needed to promote rapid growth of pollution-eating microbes.

Bioremediation of contaminated soil and groundwater occurs in two ways. In some cases, specialized microbes are added to degrade the contaminants. More commonly, ways are found to enhance the growth of whatever pollution-eating microbes might already be living at the contaminated site. Through either of these processes, cleanup can occur in place without having to remove the contaminated soil, water, or sediments.

One community in which bioremediation was used for groundwater cleanup is Hanahan, South Carolina. In 1975, about 80,000 gallons of jet fuel leaked from a storage facility. In spite of immediate cleanup efforts, some of the fuel soaked into the sandy soil and leached downward to groundwater. By 1985, the contaminated water was showing up in a nearby residential area.

Studies by the U.S. Geological Survey (USGS) indicated that naturally present soil microbes were capable of degrading the petroleum compounds into carbon dioxide and water and that this rate of biodegradation could be greatly increased if nutrients were supplied. In 1992, USGS scientists began adding nutrients to the contaminated site. By the end of 1993, the bioremediation had worked so successfully that some of the compounds were no longer detectable.

As in this story, bioremediation commonly is used to clean soils and groundwater that have been contaminated by leaking gasoline tanks or by spills of solvents, pesticides, or other toxic chemicals. By adding nutrients to the soil, it is possible to enhance the growth of naturally occurring microbes and speed up their decomposition of chemical pollutants.

Another common groundwater contaminant is tetrachloroethene, a solvent used in dry cleaning and industrial applications. When scientists at Cornell University wanted to develop a way of removing this pollutant from water, they decided to look for a strain of bacteria that would be able to eat this synthetic compound. At first, they found soil microbes that degraded tetrachloroethene into vinyl chloride, a cancer-causing compound. Clearly, this did not meet the goal of degrading the chemical into a harmless form.

Next, the scientists took samples of sludge from an old sewage treatment plant, left over from the days when dry cleaning chemicals were routinely flushed down the drain. (Flushing of dry cleaning compounds is no longer allowed—modern regulations require that they be disposed of in leak-proof containers in landfills that have been approved for hazardous waste disposal.) In the old sewage sludge, the scientists found a type of bacteria that degrades tetrachloroethene into a gas called ethylene, the natural gas that causes fruit to ripen. This was a better outcome!

Sometimes bioremediation works well in a laboratory setting but not so well when exposed to the forces of nature. So, the next step was to determine whether this strain of bacteria could break down tetrachloroethene in the environment as well as in the lab. Analysis of soils and groundwater samples showed that the tetrachloroethene-eating strain of bacteria was naturally present at contaminated sites and was capable of degrading tetrachloroethene in the field.

SCI
LINKS.
THE WORLD'S A CLICK AWAY

Topic: groundwater contaminants
Go to: www.sciLINKS.org
Code: DR08

The final step was for scientists to determine ways to speed up the growth of this strain of microbes under field conditions. They tried supplying various nutrients and found hydrogen to be the critical ingredient. By injecting hydrogen-containing compounds such as lactic acid or ethanol into contaminated sites, they were able to greatly accelerate the breakdown rate of tetrachloroethene. Armed with this information, communities now have another option to consider for cleaning up groundwater that has become contaminated with this pollutant.

CLEANING UP OIL SPILLS

When an oil spill occurs in a lake or ocean, it forms a floating layer called an oil slick. Because oil kills fish and wildlife and makes a mess of beaches and shorelines, much effort is put into cleaning up spills when they occur. Although Exxon spent over two billion dollars on cleanup operations following the 1989 Valdez spill in Alaska, thousands of seabirds and marine mammals died and long-term impacts have been measured in marine and coastal ecological communities.

Because oil and water repel each other and don't mix, even a small amount of oil can spread out over a large area. Therefore, the first strategy in cleaning up an oil spill in an ocean or lake usually is to surround the oil to try to prevent it from spreading. Then efforts are made to pump, scoop, or soak up as much of the oil as possible. The next line of attack may be to apply chemicals that break the oil into small droplets that mix with water and spread out in the environment. Some of the oil washes up on shorelines and beaches.

Bioremediation can be used to clean up oil spills or other organic pollution in water.

Photos of oil spill cleanup operations often show workers applying high-pressure sprays to wash oil from rocky shorelines and beaches (Figure 1.12). The oil that collects with the runoff water must then get scooped up or soaked up with special oil-absorbent materials.

FIGURE 1.12
High Pressure Sprays Are Used to Wash Oil-Soaked Beaches

Photo courtesy of the Alaska Resources Library and Information Services

Sometimes bioremediation is used to supplement physical and chemical cleanup strategies. On a beach or rocky shoreline, oil gradually degrades into harmless by-products such as carbon dioxide and water. This occurs over a period of years or even decades through the chemical and physical forces of weathering and the biological forces of biodegradation. Bioremediation aims to accelerate the rate at which the biodegradation occurs.

In a cup of seawater or a handful of sediment, there are countless species of microorganisms. Oil or other pollutants will kill some of these, but others will survive and grow using the pollutant as a source of food. The goal of bioremediation is to enhance the growth of this select group of pollution-eating microbes.

Experiments carried out following the Exxon Valdez oil spill showed that addition of nitrogen-containing fertilizer to rocky beaches greatly increased the natural rate of biodegradation of oil. However, Environmental Protection Agency (EPA) scientists worried that addition of fertilizers to beaches might also cause less desirable environmental impacts. Because so many different environmental factors are involved, determining the overall impact of a bioremediation project such as fertilization of oil-soaked shorelines clearly is a complicated task involving many investigations.

For example, researchers wondered whether addition of fertilizer to beaches would cause eutrophication of coastal waters by triggering excess growth of algae. To test this, scientists compared the nutrient concentrations and populations of algae in the waters just offshore from the fertilizer-treated beaches with those in control areas where no fertilizer had been added. They found no significant differences between treated and control areas, so they concluded that the fertilizer applications did not appear to be triggering excessive growth of marine algae.

Another question was whether any components of the fertilizers might be toxic to sensitive marine species. To investigate this question, scientists conducted laboratory toxicity tests called bioassays using organisms such as salmon, mussels, and oysters. (See *Assessing Toxic Risk* [2001], the first book in the Cornell Scientific Inquiry Series, and *http://ei.cornell.edu* for information about student bioassay experiments.) Some fertilizer components proved mildly toxic to oyster larvae, the most sensitive organisms tested. However, field studies led the researchers to conclude that potential impacts of fertilizer toxicity would be low because of the rapid dilution that occurs as water along treated shorelines mixes with other ocean currents.

Bioremediation is just one of many strategies for dealing with the problems associated with oil-soaked beaches and shorelines, and there is no easy solution to an environmental catastrophe of this magnitude. Of 1,100 miles of coastline impacted by the Exxon Valdez spill, only about 70 miles were treated through bioremediation. Some sites were not well-suited to this sort of treatment, others were too remote, and there simply were far too many impacted beaches for it to be feasible to apply bioremediation treatments to them all.

A decade after the Exxon Valdez spill occurred, residual oil still could be found, generally below the surface on shorelines that are sheltered from the natural weathering of wind and waves. These remaining pockets of oil will continue to break down very slowly over the years, through natural processes of biodegradation and weathering.

CHOOSING WHEN TO USE BIOREMEDIATION

Bioremediation provides a good cleanup strategy for some types of pollution, but as you might expect, it will not work for all. For example, bioremediation may not provide a feasible strategy at sites with high concentrations of chemicals that are toxic to most microorganisms. These chemicals include metals such as cadmium or lead and salts such as sodium chloride.

So, where is it appropriate to use bioremediation? It works well at sites that are contaminated with chemicals that can be used as food for at least a select group of microbes. In most cases, microbes capable of digesting the contaminant are naturally present, and the role of bioremediation is to enhance their growth by providing needed oxygen, nutrients, or moisture. In other cases specialized microbes are selected in the laboratory, then used in the field to degrade specific contaminants.

Either way, bioremediation provides a technique for cleaning up pollution by enhancing the same biodegradation processes that occur in nature. Depending on the site and its contaminants, bioremediation may be safer and less expensive than alternative solutions such as incinerating the contaminated materials or sending them to a landfill. It also has the advantage of treating the contamination in place so that large quantities of soil, sediment, or water do not have to be dug up or pumped out of the ground for treatment.

As shown in the Alaska oil spill example, an important step in choosing bioremediation strategies is to address site-specific questions concerning potential environmental impacts so that unintended side effects can be avoided.

DISCUSSION QUESTIONS

▶ What do wastewater treatment, composting, and bioremediation have in common?

▶ How can microbes get food energy from toxic chemicals such as TNT or motor oil?

▶ Why is bioremediation a useful cleanup strategy at some sites but not others?

SECTION 2

BIODEGRADATION PROTOCOLS:
INTRODUCTION TO RESEARCH

IDENTIFYING DECOMPOSERS

PROTOCOL 1. PICKING AND SORTING INVERTEBRATES

Objective

To collect and observe readily visible invertebrates in soil, compost, or decaying leaves.

Background

In a compost pile, a moist pile of leaves, or the top layers of soil in gardens, woodlands, or vacant lots, you are likely to find a wide range of invertebrates. This protocol is useful for finding large invertebrates such as earthworms, sow bugs, and centipedes. If you're interested in smaller organisms, you will find more of them using Protocol 2 or 3.

Materials (per student group)

▶ Dissecting microscope or hand lens

▶ Petri dish (for use with microscope)

▶ Light-colored tray or pan

▶ Soft tweezers or plastic spoons

▶ Jars (for temporary sorting and display of organisms)

▶ Sample of fresh soil, decaying leaves, or compost (a couple of handfuls)

▶ **Soil Invertebrate Identification Sheet** (p. 38)

Procedure

1. Collect samples of soil, decaying leaves, and/or compost.

2. Take a partially decomposed leaf and magnify it with a dissecting microscope or hand lens. Do you see any living things, or evidence that living things have been there? For example, does the leaf surface look chewed, or are there tunnels running through it?

3. Spread a thin layer of soil or compost in a light-colored tray or pan. Sort through the sample using soft tweezers, plastic spoons, or other instruments that will not hurt any organisms that may be present.

4. Gently sort organisms into jars or into a petri dish for viewing under a microscope. Using the **Soil Invertebrate Identification Sheet** for reference, collect and identify as many types of invertebrates as you can find. Use a dissecting microscope or magnifying lens to get a closer view of small organisms.

Analysis

1. Make sketches, lists, and counts of the types of organisms you have found. Then return them to the soil or compost to keep them alive.

2. Which types of organism are most abundant? If you are analyzing more than one type of sample, how do they compare? For example, in what type of sample do you find the greatest number of organisms? How about the greatest diversity?

Topic: invertebrates
Go to: www.sciLINKS.org
Code: DR09

3. Try sorting your organisms into functional groups: which ones do you think are predators, and which feed on decaying organic matter? Which group of organisms is most abundant? Sketch a food web showing possible relationships among the organisms you have found.

4. If you have access to a digital camera, you could put together an electronic presentation or picture key of the organisms you have collected.

SOIL INVERTEBRATE IDENTIFICATION SHEET
Annelids (Phylum Annelida)

Potworms (class Oligochaeta)—also known as Enchytraeids

Description: Tiny white segmented worms, 10–25 mm.

Food: Decomposing vegetation and attached bacteria and fungi.

Habitat: Damp compost or soil.

Earthworms (class Oligochaeta)

Description: Pink segmented worms, 50–150 mm. Adults have a swollen section used in mating.

Food: Decomposing vegetation and attached bacteria and fungi.

Habitat: Damp compost or soil.

Arthropods (Phylum Arthropoda)

Mites (class Arachnida)

Description: <1 mm; round body; eight legs.

Food: Some species eat organic debris such as leaf particles and rotting wood, some eat fungi or bacteria, and some are predators that eat nematodes, potworms, and other tiny organisms.

Habitat: Extremely numerous in compost piles and moist soil.

Pseudoscorpions (class Arachnida)

Description: 2–8 mm; resemble tiny scorpions, with two large pincer-like claws but without a long tail.

Food: Locate prey such as nematodes, mites, and springtails

through odor or vibrations; seize prey with powerful front claws and inject poison into victims.

Habitat: Near surface of compost or in damp leaves on forest floor.

Spiders (class Arachnida)

Description: Eight legs, up to several cm in length.

Food: Insects and other small invertebrates. Spiders inject poison and digestive juices into prey and then suck out the pre-digested body contents.

Habitat: Leaf litter and surface layers of compost.

Springtails (class Insecta)

Description: <3 mm; wingless insects with a tiny spring-like lever at the base of the abdomen.

Food: Primarily fungi and bacteria, but some species eat nematodes or detritus.

Habitat: Compost and packs of decaying leaves.

Notes: Called springtails because they catapult into the air when disturbed.

Ants (class Insecta)

Description: 5–10 mm; six legs and two short antennae.

Food: Typically eat fungi, seeds, or dead plants and animals; some prey on invertebrates.

Habitat: Found in compost during final curing phase or in surface layers of soil.

Notes: Some live in complex social structures with a queen and many workers.

Beetles (class Insecta)

Description: Hard-bodied insects with a pair of hard wings that cover softer flight wings. Common soil beetles include the rove, ground, and feather-winged beetles.

Habitat: Moist, decaying organic materials such as compost, leaf litter, and rotting logs.

Feather-winged beetles—the smallest known variety of beetles

Description: 1 mm; tiny beetles with feathery wings used for drifting in wind like dandelion seeds.

Food: Fungal spores.

Rove beetles

Description: <10 mm; usually black or brown; partially uncovered flight wings.

Food: Insects, snails, slugs, and small animals.

Ground beetles

Description: 8–20 mm; black or dark colored.

Food: Insects, snails, slugs, and small animals.

Flies (class Insecta)

Description: <10 mm; house fly larvae are soft, white, worm-like.

Food: Some types lay their eggs in decaying animals or other organic matter. The larvae, called maggots, aid in biodegradation as they feed on the decaying organic matter.

Habitat: Fruit flies, fungus gnats, and many other types of flies are common in soil and compost.

Earwigs (class Insecta)

Description: <30 mm; easily identified by jaw-like pincers at tail end.

Food: Predatory earwigs feed on insects, spiders, mites; other earwigs eat fungi, mosses, lichens, and detritus.

Habitat: Soil and compost piles.

Notes: Earwigs are active at night and hide during the day in moist, shady places.

Millipedes (class Diplopoda)

Description: 20–80 mm; cylindrical, multi-segmented body, with two pairs of legs per segment.

Food: Fungi and decaying vegetation.

Habitat: Live in and move through soil and compost.

Notes: Stink glands along their sides provide protection from predators.

Centipedes (class Chilopoda)

Description: 30 mm; flattened, segmented body, with one pair of legs per segment. The first pair of legs is modified into poisonous jaws located below the mouth.

Food: Centipedes are predators and use poison glands in their jaws to paralyze prey such as small worms, insect larvae, insects, and spiders.

Habitat: Primarily in surface layers of compost piles and soil; require moist habitat.

Sow bugs and Pill bugs (subphylum Crustacea)

Description: 10 mm; sow bugs have short, flattened gray or brown bodies with overlapping "armored" plates and one pair of legs per segment. Pill bugs, also known as "roly-polies," roll into a tight ball when disturbed.

Food: Decaying wood and resistant materials such as veins of leaves.

Habitat: Compost and forest floor. Need a moist habitat to avoid drying out.

Notes: Sow bugs and pill bugs are the only terrestrial crustaceans, related to lobsters and crabs.

Mollusks (Phylum Mollusca)

Slugs and Snails (class Gastropoda)

Description: 2–25 mm; snails have a brown or gray, soft, slimy body in a coiled shell; slugs are similar but with no shell.

Food: Living or decaying plants and fungi. Some snails and slugs secrete enzymes to pre-digest cellulose (most other invertebrates rely on bacteria in their guts to do this for them).

Habitat: Surface layers of soil or compost.

Nematodes (Phylum Nematoda)—also called Roundworms

Description: <1 mm; slender, unsegmented worms; cylindrical bodies with tapered ends; some are transparent.

Food: Bacteria, fungi, plant roots; some species prey on protozoa and other nematodes.

Habitat: Water-filled pores and thin films of water surrounding soil and compost particles.

Notes: Best viewed with a microscope. A handful of soil or compost could contain several million nematodes!

Rotifers (Phylum Rotifera)

Description: <1 mm; transparent microscopic creatures with a crown of hair-like cilia used for sweeping water and food into the mouth.

Food: Algae, decaying organic matter.

Habitat: Water-filled pores and thin films of water surrounding soil and compost particles.

Notes: Commonly found in water drained from moist soil or compost. Best viewed without a cover slip because they tend to roll up when disturbed.

Planaria (Phylum Platyhelminthes)

Description: Most are <10 mm; transparent flatworms with shovel-shaped head and two distinct eyespots.

Food: Small invertebrates, living and dead vegetation and other organic matter.

Habitat: Moist, dark, cool areas such as compost piles and rotting logs.

Notes: Commonly found in water drained from moist soil or compost.

PROTOCOL 2. BERLESE FUNNEL FOR COLLECTING INVERTEBRATES

Objective

To collect invertebrates such as mites, springtails, ants, and insect larvae that are too small to be easily found by picking and sorting through soil, compost, or decaying leaves.

Background

This protocol uses a contraption called a Berlese funnel to collect small invertebrates in a beaker or jar placed below a funnel containing soil or compost. (The Berlese [pronounced ber-lace-ee] funnel is named after Antonio Berlese, the 19th century Italian entomologist who invented it.)

Materials (per student group)

▶ Ring stand and ring

▶ Funnel lined with small piece of window screen, or kitchen sieve enclosed in paper funnel

▶ Light source (25 watt)

▶ Dissecting microscope or hand lens

▶ Sample of fresh soil or compost (a couple of handfuls)

▶ Beaker or jar

▶ Optional: 100 mL of 90% ethanol/10% glycerol solution (if you wish to preserve the collected organisms)

▶ Petri dish (for use with microscope)

▶ **Soil Invertebrate Identification Sheet** (p. 38)

Procedure

1. Assemble a funnel and sieve, either by lining the bottom of a funnel with a small piece of window screen, or by making a funnel to fit over a kitchen sieve (see Figure 2.1).

2. Into a beaker or jar, add 100 mL of water (or a mixture of 90% ethanol and 10% glycerol if you wish to preserve the organisms you collect). Place the beaker just below the funnel to collect the specimens.

3. Place soil or compost in the sieve or funnel, making a layer several centimeters deep.

4. Position a 25-watt light 2 to 5 cm above the funnel, or place the collecting apparatus in a sunny location. The light, heat, and drying will gradually

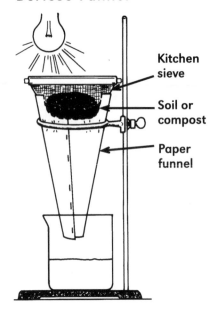

FIGURE 2.1
Berlese Funnel

Kitchen sieve

Soil or compost

Paper funnel

drive the organisms downward through the funnel and into the collecting jar. If you use too strong a light source, the organisms will dry up and die before making it through the soil and into the funnel.

5. After 2 to 24 hours, place the organisms you have collected in a petri dish, and observe them under a dissecting microscope or with a hand lens.

Analysis

Using the **Soil Invertebrate Identification Sheet** (pp. 38–41), try to identify the organisms you have found. Make sketches, lists, and counts of the various types.

1. Which types of organism are most abundant? If you are analyzing more than one type of sample, how do they compare? For example, in what type of sample do you find the greatest number of organisms? How about the greatest diversity?

2. Try sorting your organisms into functional groups. Which ones do you think are predators, and which feed on decaying organic matter? Which group of organisms is most abundant? Sketch a food web showing possible relationships among the organisms you have found.

PROTOCOL 3. WET EXTRACTION OF SOIL ORGANISMS

Objective

To collect tiny organisms such as nematodes, planaria, and protozoa that live in thin films of water surrounding particles of soil or compost.

Background

In composts and soils, microscopic films of water surround each particle, and a variety of tiny organisms live in these water films. This protocol provides a method of collecting these organisms so that you can observe them under a microscope. The wet extraction uses a device similar to the Berlese funnel in Protocol 2 except that in this case the funnel is filled with water (see Figure 2.2). As the compost or soil sample becomes saturated, the air spaces between particles fill with water. Tiny organisms such as nematodes, planaria, and protozoa swim freely in this solution. Heat and light drive them downward in the funnel, making it easy to collect them when you drain the solution into the beaker below.

Materials (per student group)

- Ring stand and attachments
- Funnel
- Rubber tubing to fit small end of funnel
- Pinch clamp
- Beaker or jar
- 5 x 5 cm square of cheesecloth
- 25 cm length of string
- Fresh sample of soil or compost (a couple of handfuls)
- Light source (25 watt)
- Light microscope
- Microscope slides and cover slips

FIGURE 2.2
Apparatus for Wet Extraction of Soil Organisms

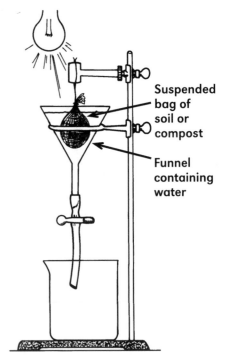

Suspended bag of soil or compost

Funnel containing water

Procedure

1. Assemble the apparatus as shown, with the funnel suspended above the beaker and the rubber tubing leading from the bottom of the funnel into the beaker. Close the tubing with a pinch clamp.

2. Collect a fresh sample of compost or soil, preferably moist so that the organisms that live in water films surrounding compost or soil particles will be in an active rather than dormant stage.

3. Make a bag of soil or compost by placing a sample on the cheesecloth, gathering the edges, and tying them tightly together at the top. The amount you use will depend on the size of your funnel (the finished bag should be small enough to fit within the funnel with space for water to flow around the edges).

4. Suspend the bag, locating it so that it hangs inside the funnel with clearance around its edges.

5. Fill the funnel with water, making sure that the soil bag is submerged but not sitting on the funnel walls.

6. Place the light above the funnel and turn it on. The light and heat will gradually drive the organisms downward in the funnel.

7. After 24 hours, open the clamp and allow the water and organisms to drain into the beaker.

Analysis

1. Observe drops of water from the collected sample under the microscope. Draw sketches of any organisms that you find.

2. Think about what roles these organisms might play in the compost or soil food web—are they producers or consumers? Do you think they eat decaying organic matter, or other organisms? Chances are good that your sample contains a wide range of consumer organisms. Together, they form the base for food webs in soil or compost. Although they are microscopic, they are so numerous that they add up to significant amounts of food energy for organisms higher in the food web and energy pyramid.

PROTOCOL 4. COLLECTING AND OBSERVING AQUATIC INVERTEBRATES

Objective

To collect samples of stream and pond invertebrates and sort them according to feeding groups and/or water quality considerations.

Background

Many types of invertebrates live in ponds and streams. Some, such as crayfish, spend their entire lives in these aquatic habitats. Others are aquatic only during their immature stages. For example, dragonflies and damselflies spend their early lives as aquatic nymphs and then emerge from the water when they become adults. During their aquatic phase, some of these invertebrates eat vegetation or decaying organic matter, and others are predators. Together they become food for fish and other higher-level consumers in aquatic food webs.

Materials (per student group)

▶ D-net or kitchen strainer

▶ Dishpan or other broad flat pan (preferably white or light-colored)

▶ 10 smaller containers such as plastic cups

▶ Soft tweezers and plastic spoons for picking up animals

▶ Hand lenses or plastic "bug boxes" with magnifying lids

▶ Latex gloves (optional, depending on the water quality)

▶ Waders, waterproof boots, or other nonslip footgear suitable for wading

▶ Other gear appropriate for the conditions (such as walking sticks to provide stability on slippery rocks or life jackets if the water is not uniformly shallow)

▶ **Stream Invertebrate Identification Sheet** (p. 49)

Procedure

Collecting Aquatic Organisms

1. Choose a safe place and time for sampling. In streams, this means choosing a site where the current is not too deep or too fast for you to have safe footing at all times. In ponds, it means choosing a shoreline where you can wade without danger of ending up in deep water.

2. You can collect stream organisms by holding a net or strainer in the current as you gently kick the rocks and stir up the sediments directly upstream. After a couple of minutes of kicking, check the net. If it contains a lot of mud, rinse it by raising and lowering in the water a few times. Then empty the contents into your dishpan, adding enough water to keep everything covered. Take a look in the pan. Any signs of life? You may need to wait a minute or so for sediments to settle before you begin to see organisms swimming or scurrying around.

3. In ponds, you can collect organisms by sweeping your net across the surface of the sediment and through the water and underwater vegetation. Empty the contents of the net by turning it inside out and gently rinsing the contents into a pan of water.

4. Another approach is to use the net to scoop up some sediment and then empty it into a pan of water. This will make the water very muddy, and you will need to wait for the mud to settle. Watch for swimming organisms, and gently pick through the sediments to find others that are hiding.

5. Another way of collecting aquatic invertebrates is to place some leaves in a mesh bag such as those in which onions are sold. Weight the bag down underwater in a stream or pond, and leave it there for a few days or weeks. When you come back, collect the bag, empty it into a dishpan of water, and investigate what sorts of organisms have moved in and begun eating the leaves.

Sorting and Observing the Organisms

1. Unless you are planning to preserve your sample organisms in alcohol, try to keep them alive so that you can return them to their natural habitat. The organisms will do best if you keep them in the shade and periodically add fresh cool water to keep the dissolved oxygen levels from dropping too low as the water warms.

2. After letting things settle for a few minutes in your pan, you can begin observing organisms. How do they move? How do they appear adapted to the habitat in which you caught them?

3. Put some fresh water into your smaller containers and begin sorting the invertebrates by appearance. You can pick them up gently with soft tweezers or scoop them up with a plastic spoon or small container. At this point, don't be too concerned with identifying the organisms, but try to sort them into groups according to their appearance.

4. Continue picking over your sample until you can't find more organisms. Look carefully for smaller and slower-moving creatures and ones that are clinging to stones or other surfaces.

5. Once you're finished sorting, observing, and sketching or describing your samples, gently pour them back into their native habitat.

Analysis

1. Write a description of your invertebrate collection, including discussion of what types of organisms you found and what feeding groups you think they represent. For example, blackfly larvae wave feathery antennae through the water to filter particles from the current. Some caddisfly larvae weave webs like spider webs attached to rock surfaces to catch particles flowing by with the current. Try finding examples in your collection that you think represent each of these functional feeding groups:

   ▶ Shredders—shred leaves or other vegetation (example: stonefly nymphs)

   ▶ Grazers—scrape algae and other food off the surfaces of rocks (example: snails)

   ▶ Collectors—gather tiny particles of organic matter from the water (example: blackfly and caddisfly larvae)

◗ Predators—catch and eat other organisms (example: dragonfly and damselfly nymphs)

Once you have sorted through your organisms, write a brief description of the roles you think they play in the processes of decay and renewal at your study site.

If you collected organisms from more than one part of the stream, how do they compare? Did you find different types of organisms in faster flowing water compared with slower areas? Can you notice any adaptations that appear to make the organisms well-suited for the habitats in which you found them?

2. If you collected organisms from a stream, you can use them to assess the water quality. Using the **Stream Invertebrate Identification Sheet** (p. 49), sort through your collection to look specifically for stoneflies, mayflies, and caddisflies. These are pollution-sensitive indicator organisms that can be used for a simple assessment of stream water quality because of their sensitivity to the concentration of dissolved oxygen. When oxygen levels drop too low, these organisms do not survive.

3. Complete Table 2.1 below to rate your study site according to the Simplified Stream Biota Test, which rates a stream site based on the presence or absence of stoneflies, mayflies, and caddisflies.

4. If you want to carry out a more thorough analysis of your collection as an indicator of stream water quality, you can find more detailed methods on the Environmental Inquiry website (*http://ei.cornell.edu*).

TABLE 2.1
Simplified Stream Biota Test

Check one cell below	Simplified Stream Biota Test A simplified method of assessing stream water quality*	
	Excellent	Stoneflies and mayflies present
	Good	Mayflies and caddisflies present, but no stoneflies
	Fair	Caddisflies present, but no stoneflies or mayflies
	Poor	No stoneflies, mayflies, or caddisflies present

*This rating system works only for rivers and streams. Pond invertebrates cannot be used to evaluate water quality because they are adapted to living with low or fluctuating dissolved oxygen concentrations.

STREAM INVERTEBRATE IDENTIFICATION SHEET

Pollution-Sensitive Organisms
—Require high dissolved oxygen levels

Stonefly nymphs (order Plecoptera)

Description: 1–4 cm; six legs, each ending in double hooks; visible antennae; two tails (never three). No gills on abdomen.

Feeding: Most species gather and eat decaying plants or animals, but some eat bacteria and others are predators.

Habitat: Swiftly moving streams with high oxygen levels.

Mayfly nymphs (order Ephemeroptera)

Description: 0.5–3 cm; six legs, each ending in a single hook; visible antennae; three long tails (sometimes two). Plate-like or feathery gills along sides of abdomen.

Feeding: Grazers or gatherers; eat algae and organic matter.

Habitat: Some cling to rocks, some burrow in mud, and others are free swimmers. Diversity of mayfly species decreases with stream degradation.

Caddisfly larvae (order Trichoptera)

Description: <2.5 cm; six legs with hooked claws; two hooks at tail end. Some species build cases of small stones or sticks, and others are free-living or spin nets attached to rocks.

Feeding: Some graze algae, others filter-feed detritus, and a few free-living species are predators.

Habitat: High-quality streams; some are tolerant of mild pollution.

Net-spinner

Case-builder

Dobsonfly larvae (order Megaloptera)—also known as "Hellgrammites"

Description: 2–10 cm; six legs; large pinching jaws; pointed feelers with feathery gills along abdomen; two tail projections, each with two hooks.

Feeding: Predators with powerful chewing mouthparts. *Caution:* If they pinch you, it hurts!

Habitat: High-quality streams.

Beetle larvae and adults (order Coleoptera)

Water penny larvae

Description: 0.5–1.25 cm; broad flat saucer-shaped body; six small legs underneath.

Feeding: Graze algae and other material attached to rocks.

Habitat: Cling to rocks in cold, fast-running, high-quality streams.

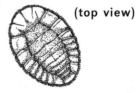

(top view)

(side view)

Riffle beetle larvae and adults

Description: Larvae are <1.25 cm; worm-like but hard body; six legs and small tuft of white filaments at tail end. Adults are 1–2 cm, black, and look similar to many terrestrial beetles.

Feeding: Collect and gather algae, diatoms, organic debris.

Habitat: Larvae cling to rocks in stream riffles. Adults walk slowly along stream bottom.

Notes: Unique in that larval and adult stages both are aquatic.

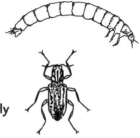

Moderately Tolerant Organisms
—Can survive with moderate oxygen levels

Fly larvae (order Diptera)

Watersnipe fly larvae

Description: <3 cm; cylindrical, slightly flattened; cone-shaped abdomen; many legs with suction tips; pale to green.

Feeding: Predators.

Habitat: Moderate quality streams and rivers.

Cranefly larvae

Description: 6 cm; large, fleshy, segmented, and worm-like, with four finger-like lobes at hind end; light brown, green, or milky color.

Feeding: Most graze on algae or are gatherers, but a few are predators.

Habitat: Can be found burrowing in mud.

Blackfly larvae

Description: <0.5 cm; head has feathery gills, tail end has suction pad.

Feeding: Filter small particles of organic matter from the current.

Habitat: Live attached to submerged rocks; require swiftly flowing water.

Damselfly and Dragonfly nymphs (order Odonata)

Damselfly nymphs

Description: 0.25–5 cm; large protruding eyes; six thin legs; long, thin, abdomen with no gills; three broad "tails" that actually are gills.

Feeding: Predators.

Habitat: Typically found in medium-quality, slowly moving water.

Dragonfly nymphs

Description: 1.25–5 cm; large protruding eyes; round to oval abdomen; six hooked legs.

Feeding: Predators; eat aquatic insects, tadpoles, and small fish.

Habitat: Slowly moving water.

Alderfly larvae (order Megaloptera)

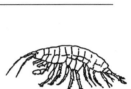

Description: <3 cm; six legs and six to eight filaments on each side of abdomen; distinguished from dobsonfly larvae by single tail projection with hairs but no hooks.

Feeding: Aggressive predators.

Habitat: High- or medium-quality water.

Scuds (order Amphipoda)

Description: <1.25 cm; swim rapidly on their sides and resemble shrimp; flat sides, hump-shaped back, and several pairs of legs; white, gray, or pink.

Feeding: Gather dead and decaying matter.

Habitat: Some highly sensitive to pollution; others found in moderately polluted water.

Crayfish (order Decapoda)

Description: <15 cm; look like small lobsters, with two large claws and eight smaller legs.

Feeding: Predators; use large claws to tear plant and animal prey into small chunks.

Habitat: Slow-moving streams, rivers, and ponds.

Pollution-Tolerant Organisms
—Can live in streams with low dissolved oxygen levels

Midge larvae (order Diptera)

Description: <1.25 cm; have a worm-like body and distinct head; often C-shaped; sometimes bright red.

Feeding: Most filter-feed or gather detritus; a few prey on other insect larvae.

Habitat: Can survive in water with low oxygen concentrations.

Aquatic worms (class Oligochaeta)

Description: Usually <7.5 cm; long, thin, segmented worms with no legs.

Feeding: Ingest mud and filter out organic material.

Habitat: Tolerant of pollution; high numbers indicate poor water quality.

Leeches (order Hirudinea)

Description: <5–8 cm; worm-like, brown, and slimy; flattened, with sucker at each end.

Feeding: Some attach suckers to prey and drink blood; others gather detritus.

Habitat: Indicators of low dissolved oxygen.

Snails (class Gastropoda)

Description: 0.5–2 cm; flat or cone-shaped shell surrounding soft body.

Feeding: Scrape algae and bacteria from surfaces of submerged rocks.

Habitat: Some species have lungs and can live in waters with low oxygen levels, and others breathe with gills and require high oxygen concentrations.

Aquatic sow bugs (order Isopoda)

Description: 0.5–2 cm; relatively flat; have long antennae and seven pairs of legs.

Feeding: Scavenge both dead and live plants and animals.

Habitat: Can tolerate high levels of decaying organic matter; typically found in muddy, slow-moving water.

Notes: Sow bugs are crustaceans, not bugs as their name suggests.

Aquatic Insect Life Cycles—Larvae vs. Nymphs

You may be wondering why some immature organisms are called "larvae" and others are called "nymphs." The answer has to do with the type of metamorphosis they undergo to become adults.

Insects such as blackflies go through complete metamorphosis, with four stages, and their immature forms are called larvae:

Egg → Larva

↑ ↓

Adult ← Pupa

Others such as dragonflies undergo incomplete metamorphosis, with only three stages, and their immature forms are called nymphs:

Egg

Adult ← Nymph

PROTOCOL 5. OBSERVING SOIL MICROORGANISMS

Objective

To make simple observations of the microbial communities in soil or compost.

Background

Microorganisms live in every conceivable habitat, from frozen glaciers to scalding thermal springs. Bacteria and fungi are the most abundant living things on earth, and they also play the most significant roles in biodegradation. Under a microscope, you're likely to see a wide range of microbial life in any sample of soil or compost. Staining helps to highlight bacteria so that you can observe them in greater detail.

Materials (per student group)

▶ Compound microscope with a 100X oil immersion lens

▶ Microscope slides and cover slips

▶ Eye dropper

▶ A few drops 0.85% NaCl (saline solution)* or water

▶ Toothpick

▶ A handful of fresh soil, compost, or decaying leaves

For bacterial staining (optional)

▶ Methylene blue solution* (Loeffler's bacterial stain)

▶ Distilled water

▶ Bunsen burner

▶ Toothpick

▶ Blotting paper or filter paper

Procedure

1. Make a wet mount by putting a drop of saline solution or water on a microscope slide and transferring a small amount of soil, compost, or decaying leaf to the drop. (If you add too much, it will block the light that needs to pass through the slide for viewing.)

2. Using a toothpick, stir the sample into the water or saline solution (the preparation should be watery), and apply a cover slip.

3. Observe under low and high power. You might be able to see many nematodes squirming and thrashing around. Other possibilities include planaria, rotifers, mites, springtails, and protozoa. Strands of fungi may be visible but difficult to recognize because the long filaments will probably not remain intact. Bacteria appear as very tiny, round particles that seem to be vibrating in the background.

---

* The *Teacher Edition* includes instructions for making the saline and methylene blue solutions.

4. Prepare stained slides if you want to highlight bacteria to observe them in greater detail:

   a. Using a toothpick, mix a small amount of soil with a drop of saline solution on a slide, and spread it into a thin layer.

   b. Let the mixture air-dry until a white film appears on the slide.

   c. Heat-fix the bacteria to the slide by passing the slide through a hot flame several times.

   d. Stain the slide by covering it with the methylene blue stain for one minute. Rinse the slide with distilled water and gently blot it dry using blotting or filter paper.

Analysis

Sketch and describe the microorganisms on your slides. Bacteria make up 80 to 90% of the billions of microorganisms typically found in a gram of compost. They are single-celled and shaped like tiny rods, spheres, or spirals. Some have the ability to move under their own power.

Rods   Spheres   Spirals

Fungi grow long thin filaments, sometimes tangled together in mats.

Fungi

However, thread-like branched filaments also might belong to a type of bacteria called actinomycetes, which are important decomposers that contribute to the earthy smell of compost. The filaments are about 10 times thinner than those of fungi, and they look like spider webs stretching through compost. Actinomycetes can most easily be seen in the outer edges of the pile during the early stages of the composting process.

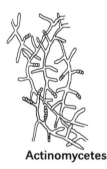

Actinomycetes

What types of bacteria did you find? If you have made slides from more than one type of sample, how do they compare? Is this what you expected?

PROTOCOL 6. CULTURING BACTERIA

Objective

To grow bacterial cultures, count colonies, and observe them under the microscope.

Background

This protocol provides instructions for growing lab cultures of soil bacteria. It uses a culture medium that provides moisture and the essential nutrients to support a wide range of bacterial species.

Photo by Elaina Olynciw

Materials (per student group)

▶ Balance (to measure 5 g sample)

▶ Incubator (optional)

▶ Compound microscope with a 100X oil immersion lens

▶ Bunsen burner

▶ Matches or striker

▶ Disinfectant solution such as a household cleaning solution

▶ 5 g fresh sample of soil or compost

▶ 90 mL phosphate buffer solution with a pH of 7.6 (sterile)*

▶ 5 test tubes with caps (sterile)

▶ 1 10-mL pipette (sterile)

▶ 5 1-mL pipettes (sterile)

▶ 3 0.1-mL pipettes (sterile)

▶ Pipette bulb or pump

▶ 3 petri dishes containing TSA agar (sterile)*

▶ 3 bacteriological spreading rods or cotton swabs (sterile)

▶ Glass marker or tape for labels

▶ Goggles

▶ Gloves

For making and observing slides

▶ Microscope slides

▶ Inoculating loop or toothpick

▶ Saline solution

SCiLINKS
THE WORLD'S A CLICK AWAY

Topic: bacteria
Go to: *www.sciLINKS.org*
Code: DR10

---

* The *Teacher Edition* includes instructions for making TSA agar, phosphate buffer solution, and methylene blue solution and for maintaining sterile conditions and disposing of microbiological cultures.

For bacterial staining (optional)

▶ Methylene blue solution (Loeffler's bacterial stain) (see footnote, p. 55)

▶ Distilled water

▶ Blotting paper or filter paper

Procedure

1. Wearing goggles and gloves, wipe down your work area with disinfectant solution.

2. Use a 10 mL sterile pipette to transfer 9 mL phosphate buffer solution into each of five sterile test tubes.

3. To the 45 mL phosphate buffer solution remaining in the flask, add 5 g soil or compost and swirl vigorously.

4. The next step is to perform serial dilutions of the soil/buffer mixture in order to dilute the concentrations of bacteria (Figure 2.3). Culture plates grown from the most concentrated solutions are likely to contain many bacterial colonies growing on top of each other. For better observations, you want to achieve a concentration in which the colonies are spread out. Make serial dilutions to the 10^{-7} concentration as follows:

   a. Label the five sterile test tubes containing sterilized phosphate buffer solution: 10^{-2}, 10^{-3}, 10^{-4}, 10^{-5}, and 10^{-6}.

   b. The mixture in the flask is a 10^{-1} dilution, because 5 g soil are mixed with 45 mL solution (which is equivalent to 45 g). Mix the soil/buffer solution so that the solids become suspended. Using a 1 mL sterile pipette, transfer 1 mL of this mixture into the first test tube, labeled 10^{-2}.

   c. Mix thoroughly, then use another 1 mL sterile pipette to transfer 1 mL of the solution in the 10^{-2} test tube to the one labeled 10^{-3}. The solution in each test tube will be ten times more dilute than the previous solution from which it was made.

   d. Continue with this sequence until all five test tubes have been inoculated, each time using a sterile pipette.

   e. Label three petri dishes with the type of compost, date, and dilution: 10^{-5}, 10^{-6}, and 10^{-7}.

   f. Using a 0.1 mL sterile pipette, transfer 0.1 mL from the 10^{-4} test tube onto the agar in the petri dish labeled 10^{-5}. Spin the dish and spread the liquid as evenly as possible using a sterile spreading rod. Follow this same procedure using 0.1 mL from the 10^{-5} test tube into the dish labeled 10^{-6}, and so forth until all dilutions have been plated. For each dilution, use a sterile pipette and spreading rod.

FIGURE 2.3
Serial Dilution of Bacteria

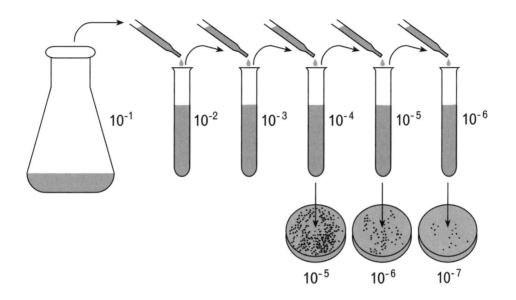

5. Cover the petri dishes and turn them upside down so that any water that condenses will not drip into the cultures. Incubate them at 28°C if possible. (If you do not have access to an incubator, room temperature is acceptable but avoid direct sunlight.)

6. After two to three days, take a look at your plates. You are likely to see many tiny dots, each of which is a colony that contains millions of bacteria. Choose a plate that has a variety of colonies but not so many that they are crowded on top of each other. (Remember, this is why you did the serial dilution—so you would have a range of densities to choose from.) Count the colonies on the plate you have chosen, and try to figure out how many different types of bacteria are represented.

7. Individually, bacteria are much too small to see without a microscope, so the next step is to prepare microscopic slides. Depending on how much time is available, choose one or more colonies to look at under the microscope. For each colony chosen, follow these steps:

   a. Use an inoculating loop or toothpick to add a drop of saline to a clean slide.

   b. Dip the loop or toothpick into a single bacterial colony and then mix it into the saline solution.

   c. Let the slide air-dry until a white film appears.

   d. Heat-fix the slide by passing it through a flame a few times.

8. If you want to highlight bacteria to observe them in greater detail, stain the slide by covering it with methylene blue solution for one minute, then rinse with distilled water and gently blot dry using blotting or filter paper.

Analysis

Observe your slides under the microscope and make sketches of what you see.

Most bacteria look like one of the following shapes:*

Rods

Spheres

Spirals

Which shapes do you see on your slides? Do you find different shapes of bacteria in the different types of colonies?

If you or your classmates have cultured different types of samples, such as soils taken at various depths or sampling locations, then you will be able to compare the abundance and types of bacteria. To analyze abundance, take a look at the petri dishes and compare how many colonies grew at the same dilution level from one type of sample to the next.

---

*Actinomycetes, bacteria with long, thread-like filaments similar to spider webs, are not likely to show up using this protocol because they take up to two weeks to grow and do better with a culture medium designed to inhibit growth of other types of bacteria. For instructions on culturing actinomycetes, see pp. 60–61 of *Composting in the Classroom: Scientific Inquiry for High School Students*, by N. M. Trautmann and M. E. Krasny. 1998. (Dubuque, IA: Kendall/Hunt. ISBN 0-7872-4433-3).

PROTOCOL 7. CULTURING FUNGI

Objective

To make cultures of fungi, count colonies and observe them under the microscope.

Background

This protocol is similar to Protocol 6 but uses a different culture medium because fungi grow better in a more acidic environment than bacteria.

Photo by Elaina Olynciw

Materials (per student group)

▶ Incubator (optional)

▶ Microscope

▶ Bunsen burner

▶ Matches or striker

▶ Disinfectant solution such as a household cleaning solution

▶ 5 g fresh sample of soil or compost

▶ 72 mL phosphate buffer solution (sterile)*

▶ 3 test tubes with caps (sterile)

▶ 3 petri dishes containing PDA agar (sterile)*

▶ 1 10-mL pipette (sterile)

▶ 3 1-mL pipettes (sterile)

▶ 3 0.1-mL pipettes (sterile)

▶ Pipette bulb or pump

▶ 3 bacteriological spreading rods or cotton swabs (sterile)

▶ Goggles

▶ Gloves

For making and observing slides

▶ Scalpel

▶ Microscope slides and cover slips

*The *Teacher Edition* includes instructions for making phosphate buffer solution and PDA agar, maintaining sterile conditions, and disposing of microbiological cultures when you are finished with them.

Procedure

1. Wearing goggles and gloves, wipe down your work area with disinfectant solution.

2. Use a 10 mL sterile pipette to transfer 9 mL buffer stock solution into each of three sterile test tubes.

3. To the 45 mL buffer stock solution remaining in the flask, add 5 g soil or compost and swirl vigorously.

4. The next step is to perform serial dilutions of this mixture in order to dilute the concentration of fungal cells (Figure 2.4). Culture plates grown from the most concentrated solutions are likely to contain many fungal colonies growing on top of each other. For better observations, you want to achieve a concentration in which the colonies are spread out. Make serial dilutions to the 10^{-5} concentration as follows:

   a. Label three test tubes: 10^{-2}, 10^{-3}, and 10^{-4}.

   b. The mixture in the flask is a 10^{-1} dilution, because 5 g compost are mixed with 45 mL solution (which is equivalent to 45 g). Mix the soil/buffer solution so that the solids become suspended. Using a 1 mL sterile pipette, transfer 1 mL of this mixture into the first test tube, labeled 10^{-2}.

   c. Mix thoroughly, then use another 1 mL sterile pipette to transfer 1 mL of the solution from the 10^{-2} test tube to the one labeled 10^{-3}. The solution in each test tube will be ten times more dilute than the previous solution from which it was made.

   d. Continue with this sequence until all three test tubes have been inoculated, each time using a sterile pipette.

   e. Label three petri dishes with the type of compost, date, and dilution: 10^{-3}, 10^{-4}, and 10^{-5}.

   f. Using a 0.1 mL sterile pipette, transfer 0.1 mL from the 10^{-2} test tube onto the agar in the petri dish labeled 10^{-3}. Spin the dish and spread the liquid as evenly as possible using a sterile spreading rod. Follow this same procedure using 0.1 mL from the 10^{-3} test tube into the dish labeled 10^{-4}, and so forth until all dilutions have been plated. For each dilution, use a sterile pipette and spreading rod.

FIGURE 2.4
Serial Dilution of Fungi

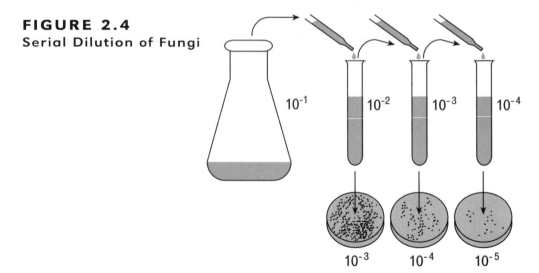

5. Cover the petri dishes and turn them upside down so that any water that condenses will not drip into the cultures. Incubate them at 28°C if possible. (If you do not have access to an incubator, room temperature is acceptable but avoid direct sunlight.)

6. After three to four days, take counts and samples of fungal colonies. Using a scalpel, lift a portion of a fungal colony intact onto a clean slide (it will still be attached to the agar) and add a cover slip.

Analysis

Observe your slides under the microscope, especially at the edges of the sample where it will be thin enough for light to pass through. Make a sketch of what you see.

What shapes do you see? Can you find long branching filaments? If you have also made slides of bacteria (Protocol 6), how do these compare with the fungi?

If you or your classmates have cultured different types of samples, such as samples taken at various depths in a compost pile or at various times during the composting process, then you will be able to compare the abundance and types of fungi. To analyze abundance, take a look at the petri dishes and compare how many colonies grew at the same dilution level from one type of sample to the next. How do these results compare with your predictions?

CHEMICAL EFFECTS OF BIODEGRADATION

PROTOCOL 8. MEASURING CO$_2$ PRODUCED IN SOIL OR COMPOST

Objective

To determine decomposition rates in soil or compost by measuring the amount of carbon dioxide (CO$_2$) given off over a two-day period.

Background

When microbes and other organisms in soil or compost use organic matter as food, they produce carbon dioxide through the process of respiration:

organic matter + oxygen → carbon dioxide + water + energy

Measurements of the rate at which carbon dioxide gets released into the air therefore can be used to estimate the rate of biodegradation. In this protocol, a chemical called soda lime is used to absorb CO$_2$ gas. Using this protocol, you can carry out experiments to compare the rates of biodegradation in soils from various locations or sampling depths, to trace the composting process over time, or to test whether compost samples are stable and ready for use.

This protocol involves three steps: Taking samples (Protocol 8a), determining the moisture content (Protocol 8b), and measuring the rate of CO$_2$ production (Protocol 8c).

PROTOCOL 8A. TAKING SAMPLES

This protocol describes how to take samples of compost, soil, or the layer of decaying leaves at the soil surface.

Materials (per student group)

▶ Soil corer, or knife and jar lid 8–10 cm in diameter

▶ Rubber spatula or trowel

▶ Plastic wrap or plastic bags

▶ Plastic container with holes and lid for storing samples

Procedure

1. *Sampling compost:* Keep in mind that decomposition tends to be slower in the outer edges of the pile because of the dryer and cooler conditions there. To get a sample that is representative of the pile as a whole, you therefore should sample at various depths, and it is best to take several samples and mix them together.

2. *Sampling leaf litter:* If you want to study biodegradation in nature, one good place to look is the layer of decaying vegetation and the top few centimeters of soil in a wooded area. First brush away any dry leaves and then take your sample from the flattened mat of damp vegetation and surface soil, using the procedure described in Step 3 below.

3. *Sampling soil:* Before taking soil samples, you must first decide the purpose of your sampling. For example, do you plan to compare soils from various locations or from various depths at a single site? Soils vary with depth, so the depth of sampling is an important consideration. In undisturbed soils, the surface layers are likely to be deep brown or black because of their high organic matter content. This is where you would expect the rates of biological activity to be the highest. Deeper soils are likely to be gray or light brown because they contain much less organic matter and therefore support less life.

   To sample the soil, start by scraping away any leaves or other plant materials at the ground surface. If you have access to a scientific soil corer or a garden tool designed for planting spring bulbs, you can use it to extract a soil core. Otherwise, using a jar lid or other hard, round object as a guide, you can make a round core by cutting into the soil to whatever depth is appropriate for your experiment. Using a coring tool, trowel, or a rubber spatula, carefully lift the soil core out of the ground, trying to preserve the various layers, and keep the core intact because microbial activity depends on the soil structure.

4. Wrap each sample in plastic wrap or place it in a plastic bag and label it. Place in a storage container. Proceed with determining soil moisture (Protocol 8b) and then with CO$_2$ measurements (Protocol 8c).

PROTOCOL 8B. DETERMINING SOIL MOISTURE CONTENT

Introduction

If you want to measure the rate at which carbon dioxide is released from soil or compost, you may be wondering why you need to start by measuring the moisture content. One reason is that it allows you to calculate the dry weight of your sample, a number that is used in the formula for determining the rate of CO$_2$ production.

Another reason is that moisture greatly affects the rate of growth of soil microbes. Slightly moist conditions provide the best environment. If soil or compost becomes too dry, the microbes become dormant. When conditions are too wet, lack of air creates an environment in which only microbes that don't need oxygen can survive. By measuring the moisture content of a subsample, you can determine if you have to add water to your larger sample, if you should allow it to dry out, or if it already has the right moisture conditions for optimal microbial growth and biodegradation.

Materials (per soil sample)

- Metric balance with 0.01 g accuracy
- Drying oven or microwave
- 10–20 g soil sample
- Beaker
- Spoon or scoopula for handling soil
- Distilled or unchlorinated water (if needed for Part 2)
- **Soil Moisture Content Data Form** (p. 69)

Procedure

Part 1. Determine % moisture, using a subsample

In this procedure you will use a subsample of your soil or compost so that you will still have some left to measure CO$_2$ production. All weights should be measured to the nearest 0.1 gram. For simplicity in the following directions, we refer to soil, but your sample could be compost instead.

1. Thoroughly mix your entire soil sample and remove any large chunks such as pebbles or roots. Fill in the top section of the **Soil Moisture Content Data Form,** then use the form to record the measurements and calculations you make in the following steps.

2. Label and record the weight of a small beaker.

3. Weigh 10–20 g of your soil directly into the beaker. Record the exact weight of the beaker and soil. Subtract out the weight of the beaker to determine the weight of the soil. (This is the wet weight.)

$$\text{wet wt of soil} \quad = \quad \begin{array}{c} \text{combined wt} \\ \text{of beaker and soil} \end{array} \quad - \quad \text{wt of beaker}$$

4. Dry the soil using either a drying oven or microwave. If using a drying oven, dry the sample for 24 hours at about 100°C. If using a microwave oven, drying time will vary. First heat the sample on LOW power for five minutes, allow to cool, and then weigh it. (It is essential to use low power so that the soils do not reach a high enough temperature to burn or release anything other than water.) Then keep heating for one additional minute and weigh the sample at each interval. Repeat this cycle until the weight change before and after heating is minimal.

5. After drying, record the weight of the beaker and the soil. Subtract out the weight of the beaker to determine the weight of the soil. (This is the dry weight.)

$$\text{dry wt of subsample} \quad = \quad \begin{array}{c} \text{combined wt of beaker} \\ \text{and soil after drying} \end{array} \quad - \quad \text{wt of beaker}$$

6. Calculate the moisture content using the following equation:

$$\text{moisture content} = \frac{\text{wet wt} - \text{dry wt}}{\text{wet wt}}$$

This result is expressed in decimal form for use in dry weight and CO_2 calculations. To express as a percentage instead, simply multiply by 100.

7. If the soil contains more than 90% water, it is too wet. Spread your larger sample out in a thin layer, and allow it to dry at room temperature out of direct sunlight until it looks moist but not wet. Repeat Steps 2–6 with a new subsample after the soil has dried, to determine if the desired moisture content has been reached. If the soil is still too wet, continue the drying process until the moisture content is near 50%.

8. If the soil contains less than 10% moisture, follow Part 2 below to figure out how much water to add.

9. If the soil is in the 10–90% moisture range, proceed to Protocol 8c to measure the CO_2 production rate.

Part 2. Adjust total sample to 50% moisture (Perform only if soil moisture content is <10%: see Step 7 above)

In Part 2 your calculations and adjustments will be for your full sample (not the subsample used in Part 1 above).

1. Weigh your total soil sample. This is the *total soil weight.*

2. Calculate the actual water weight in your total sample using the % moisture you determined in Part 1.

$$\begin{array}{ccc}
\text{actual water wt} & & \text{total soil wt of} \\
\text{of full sample} & = & \text{full sample}
\end{array} \times \begin{array}{c}
\text{moisture content} \\
\text{of the subsample}
\end{array}$$

3. Find the total *dry* weight of your soil sample.

$$\begin{array}{ccc}
\text{dry wt of full} & & \text{total soil wt of} \\
\text{sample} & = & \text{full sample}
\end{array} - \begin{array}{c}
\text{actual water wt} \\
\text{of full sample}
\end{array}$$

4. For a 50% moisture sample, the desired water weight is equal to the dry weight of the sample. If your % moisture is too low, determine how much water you need to add by using this calculation:

$$\begin{array}{ccc}
\text{wt of water} & & \text{desired} \\
\text{to be added} & = & \text{water wt}
\end{array} - \begin{array}{c}
\text{actual} \\
\text{water wt}
\end{array}$$

5. Add the amount of water needed. If possible, use distilled or bottled water, especially if your tap water contains chlorine. To weigh water, first weigh a beaker and then slowly add water until you have the correct weight (beaker + water - beaker).

6. Gently sprinkle the calculated amount of water into the entire soil sample, and mix thoroughly.

7. Let the soil sit for 24 hours to allow microorganisms to regain activity before beginning Protocol 8c to measure the rate of CO$_2$ production.

PROTOCOL 8C. MEASURING THE RATE OF CO$_2$ PRODUCTION

Introduction

CO$_2$ is produced in soil or compost through respiration by soil organisms as they use available organic material for food. The rate at which CO$_2$ is released therefore provides an indication of the rate at which decomposition is occurring. In this protocol, soda lime is used to absorb CO$_2$ from the air. The change in weight of the soda lime indicates the amount of CO$_2$ released from the soil or compost sample over the 48-hour exposure period.

Soda lime is made of sodium hydroxide (NaOH) and calcium hydroxide (Ca(OH)$_2$). When exposed to air, it undergoes the following reactions:

$$2 \text{ NaOH} + \text{CO}_2 \rightarrow \text{Na}_2\text{CO}_3 + \text{H}_2\text{O}$$
$$\text{Ca(OH)}_2 + \text{CO}_2 \rightarrow \text{CaCO}_3 + \text{H}_2\text{O}$$

As the above equations indicate, when soda lime reacts with CO$_2$, it gains weight from the formation of Na$_2$CO$_3$, CaCO$_3$, and water. However, soda lime also absorbs moisture from the air, which has nothing to do with the CO$_2$ production rate. To correct for this weight gain due to atmospheric water, the soda lime will be dried at the end of the protocol. Because this evaporates both the absorbed water and the water produced during the CO$_2$ reaction, the weight of the dry soda lime underestimates the total weight gain caused by CO$_2$. To correct for this, you will need to multiply the dry soda lime weight gain by a correction factor of 1.69.

To correct for atmospheric CO$_2$, you will create a blank by placing soda lime in an airtight container with no soil sample and then follow the same procedures as those used for the soil samples. The "blank" soda lime will tell you how much CO$_2$ was in the air when the containers were first sealed. You will subtract this from the results you get from the containers of soil samples.

Materials (per soil sample or blank)

▶ Metric balance with 0.01 g accuracy

▶ Drying oven or microwave

▶ Fresh soil sample (enough to cover airtight container to a depth of 1 cm)

▶ 1 shallow, airtight container for each soil sample (approximately 25 x 25 cm)

▶ 1 glass petri dish or watch glass (microwave-proof)

▶ 20 g soda lime

▶ Spoon or scoopula for handling soda lime

▶ Goggles

▶ Gloves

▶ **Data Form for Blanks** (1 copy for each blank) (p. 71)

▶ **Data Form for Samples** (1 copy for each sample) (p. 72)

▶ **Summary Data Form** (1 copy per treatment) (p. 74)

Procedure

There are four parts of this procedure: creating blanks, preparing the soil samples, preparing the soda lime, and incubating the samples with the soda lime. Note that you need to have the soil samples and soda lime ready to be put together in the airtight container at the same time. Therefore, after preparing the soil samples, prepare the soda lime immediately. The changes in soda lime weight will be very small (in the order of tenths of a gram). Therefore, it is essential that you follow the instructions exactly, being careful to obtain and record accurate weights and to time the steps as specified.

Part 1. Create blanks

For every five soil samples you should create one blank. Follow the directions below except do not use any soil and you do not need to record the weight of the airtight container. Simply place a dried dish of soda lime into an empty airtight container like the ones you are using for soil samples, then label and seal it. Place this empty container with the others, and after 48 hours, follow Steps 2–4 in Part 4, Incubate Soils with Soda Lime, below. The *blank soda lime weight gain* that you calculate will account for the background level of CO_2 in the air.

Part 2. Prepare soil samples

1. Just before measuring the dry weight of the soda lime, mix the soil thoroughly.

2. Record the weight of the airtight container (without lid) to the nearest 0.1 g.

3. Spread each soil sample in an airtight container to approximately 1 cm thickness. Record the weight of the soil and container to the nearest 0.1 g. For each sample, fill out the top section of the **Data Form for Samples.**

Part 3. Prepare soda lime

NOTE: Before beginning this section of the protocol, put on gloves and protective eyewear.

1. Record the weight of a petri dish bottom to the nearest 0.01g.

2. Add about 20 g of soda lime to the petri dish and leave uncovered. If you will be measuring CO$_2$ respiration for several soil samples, try to use the same amount of soda lime for each (within 0.5 g). Record the weight of the soda lime and petri dish to the nearest 0.01 g.

3. Dry the petri dish with the soda lime in a microwave or drying oven. If using a drying oven, the sample should be dried for 24 hours at 100°C. If using a microwave, heat the sample for two minutes on LOW power. Weigh it. Heat for an additional minute. Weigh the sample again. Repeat this cycle until the change in weight before and after heating is minimal.

4. Immediately after drying the soda lime, record the dry weight of the soda lime and petri dish bottom to the nearest 0.01 g. Since soda lime absorbs water from the air, it should be used immediately after completing this step.

Part 4. Incubate soils with soda lime

1. Place the uncovered petri dish and soda lime gently on the soil in one corner of the container. Place the lid on the container and make an airtight seal, being careful not to spill any soda lime out of the petri dish. Allow it to sit for 48 hours at room temperature out of direct sunlight.

2. After 48 hours, remove the dish containing soda lime. Brush off any soil that is stuck to the outside of the petri dish, then dry the soda lime again, either in a drying oven for 24 hours at ~100°C or in a microwave (see Step 3 under Prepare Soda Lime, above).

Part 5. Calculate the amount of CO$_2$ produced

(These calculations can be carried out on the data forms.)

1. Immediately after drying, measure the combined weight of the dried soda lime and petri dish to the nearest 0.01 g.

2. Subtract the weight of the dried soda lime before the 48-hour incubation period from the weight of the dried soda lime after the incubation period. This will be a very small number and is known as the *sample soda lime weight gain.*

$$\text{sample soda lime wt gain} = \text{wt of dried soda lime after incubation with soil} - \text{wt of dried soda lime before incubation}$$

3. The soda lime weight gain of the blank is referred to below as the *blank soda lime weight gain.* If your soda lime blank decreased or did not gain any weight, this means your ambient CO2 levels were very small, and your blank soda lime weight gain is zero. If you used more than one blank, calculate the average blank soda lime weight gain and use it below.

$$\text{blank soda lime wt gain} = \text{wt of dried soda lime after incubation without soil} - \text{wt of dried soda lime before incubation}$$

4. For samples, calculate the corrected soda lime weight gain using the following formula:

**corrected soda lime   =   sample soda lime   −   blank soda lime
wt gain   wt gain   wt gain**

5. Calculate the total dry weight of the soil you used.

dry wt = total soil wt − (moisture content x total soil wt)

For example, if the moisture content of a soil sample weighing 20 grams is 60%, then:

dry wt = 20 grams − (0.60 x 20 grams) = 8 g

6. The amount of CO_2 produced can be calculated using the following formula:

$$CO_2 \text{ respiration} = \frac{(\text{milligrams } CO_2) \times 1.69 / (\text{\# of days})}{(\text{kilograms dry soil})}$$

(Multiplying by 1.69 corrects for evaporation of the water produced during the reaction of soda lime and CO_2. See the introduction to Protocol 8c for an explanation.)

If you plan to repeat this protocol, you can keep reusing the same soda lime until it has increased by about 7% of its original mass. After this occurs, new soda lime should be used.

Data Analysis and Interpretation

For each sample, calculate the CO_2 production rate using the **Data Form for Samples**. Compile all of your data on the **Summary Data Form**, and calculate average CO_2 production rates among replicates of each type of sample or treatment. For example, if you tested several types of compost, calculate an average production rate for each type.

Use the questions on the **Summary Data Form** to guide your interpretation of your results.

MEASURING CO$_2$ PRODUCTION USING SODA LIME: *SOIL MOISTURE CONTENT DATA FORM*

For use with Protocol 8b: Determining Soil Moisture Content
Complete one form for each soil sample.

Name(s) _____ Date _____

Soil sample ID number_____

Soil sampling location _____

Type of area sampled (e.g., forest, schoolyard) _____

_____

Date soil sample was collected _____

Describe the soil sample (e.g., number and size of rocks and roots in sample; did the soil appear to be very wet or very dry?)

Was the soil sample well mixed? _____

Date and time soil subsample placed in drying oven_____

Date and time soil subsample removed from drying oven_____

or, time and power level required to dry subsample in microwave _____

Protocol 8B, Part 1: Determine % moisture, using a subsample.

Step 2:

Weight of beaker   = _____ g

Step 3:

wet wt of soil   = combined wt of beaker and soil   – wt of beaker

       = _____ g   – _____ g

       = _____ g

Step 5:

dry wt of subsample   = combined wt of beaker and soil after drying   – wt of beaker

       = _____ g   – _____ g

       = _____ g

Step 6:

$$\text{Moisture content} = \frac{\text{wet wt - dry wt}}{\text{wet wt}} = \frac{g - g}{g}$$

Moisture content = _____

This result is expressed in decimal form for use in dry weight and CO_2 calculations. To express as a percentage instead, simply multiply by 100.

Protocol 8B, Part 2: Adjust total sample to 50% moisture, if needed.

Step 1:

Total soil weight = _____ g

Step 2:

actual water wt of full sample	=	total soil wt of full sample	x	moisture content of subsample
	=	_____ g	x	_____ g
	=	_____ g		

Step 3:

dry wt of full sample	=	total soil wt of full sample	−	actual water wt of full sample
	=	_____ g	−	_____ g
	=	_____ g		

Step 4:

wt of water to be added	=	desired water wt	−	actual water wt
	=	_____ g	−	_____ g
	=	_____ g		

MEASURING CO$_2$ PRODUCTION USING SODA LIME:
DATA FORM FOR BLANKS

For use with Protocol 8C: Measuring the Rate of CO$_2$ Production
Complete this form for each blank.

Name(s) _____

Date _____

Protocol 8C, Part 3: Prepare soda lime.

Before incubation:

Weight of petri dish bottom   = _____ g

Weight of dish and soda lime before drying   = _____ g

Weight of dish and soda lime after drying (**A**)   = _____ g

Protocol 8C, Part 5: Calculate the amount of CO$_2$ produced.

After incubation:

Weight of dish and soda lime   = _____ g

Weight of dish and soda lime after re-drying (**B**) = _____ g

Blank soda lime weight gain (C)   = **B** – **A** = _____ g

MEASURING CO$_2$ PRODUCTION USING SODA LIME: *DATA FORM FOR SAMPLES*

For use with Protocol 8C: Measuring the Rate of CO₂ Production
Complete this form for each soil sample.

Name(s) _____

Today's date _____ Sampling date_____

Soil sampling ID number _____

Soil sampling location _____

Type of area sampled (such as forest or field) _____

Soil description _____

Date and time soda lime incubation started _____

Date and time soda lime incubation ended _____

Total # days incubation (should be two days) _____

Protocol 8C, Part 2: Prepare soil samples.

Before incubation:

Weight of container (without lid) (**G**) = _____ g

Weight of container (without lid) and soil (**H**) = _____ g

Total soil wt (I) = H – G = _____ g

Protocol 8C, Part 3: Prepare soda lime.

Before incubation:

Weight of petri dish bottom = _____ g

Weight of dish and soda lime before drying = _____ g

Weight of dish and soda lime after drying (**J**) = _____ g

Protocol 8C, Part 5: Calculate the amount of CO₂ produced.

After incubation and re-drying of the soda lime:

Weight of dish and soda lime = _____ g

Weight of dish and soda lime after re-drying (**K**) = _____ g

Sample soda lime wt gain (L) = **K – J** = _____ g

MEASURING CO$_2$ PRODUCTION USING SODA LIME: *DATA FORM FOR SAMPLES (continued)*

Calculating the rate of CO$_2$ production

1. Calculate the corrected weight gain for soda lime:

corrected soda lime wt gain	=	sample soda lime wt gain	−	blank soda lime wt gain
Y	=	**L**	−	**C**
_____ g	= _____ g		− _____ g	

The answer will be in grams of CO$_2$ produced. For use in the final equation, you'll need to convert this to milligrams:

_____ g x 1000 mg/g = _____ mg CO$_2$

2. Calculate the dry weight of the total soil sample (using soil weights from this form and % moisture content from Part 1, Step 6 on the **Data Form for Soil Moisture Content**):

Dry weight = total soil wt − (moisture content x total soil wt)

Z = I − (moisture content x I)

_____ g = _____ g − (_____ x _____ g)

This answer will be in grams of dry soil. For use in the final equation, you'll need to convert it to kilograms:

_____ g x 0.001 kg/g = _____ kg dry soil

3. Calculate the rate of CO$_2$ production in milligrams CO$_2$ produced per day per kilogram of dry soil. Use your answers from the previous two steps in place of the Y and Z in this equation:

$$\text{CO}_2 \text{ production rate} = \frac{\text{Y mg CO}_2 \text{ x } 1.69/2 \text{ days}}{\text{Z kg dry soil}} = \text{_____ mg CO}_2/\text{day/kg dry soil}$$

NOTE: If your exposure time was not two days, replace the two in this equation with the correct # days.

MEASURING CO_2 PRODUCTION USING SODA LIME: *SUMMARY DATA FORM*

Use this form to compile results from all of your samples.

Name(s) _____ Date _____

Date soil samples were collected _____

Describe the soil or compost samples listed on this page. Include soil sampling location, a description of the location, and any other useful information (such as sampling depth or observations about soil conditions at the sampling site).

If you carried out an experiment using treatments, such as worms vs. no worms, describe your treatments here.

Summarize your data in the table below (this may include relevant data from other students as well as your own). Use the numbers that you calculated on the **Data Form for Samples** to fill in Columns 3–5. The final column is for display of mean CO_2 production rates among replicate samples. If you carried out an experiment with treatments, then you will calculate separate means for each treatment.

Soil sample ID#	Treatment or type of sample	Corrected soda lime weight gain (mg CO_2)	Total soil sample dry weight (kg)	CO_2 production rate (mg CO_2/ day/kg dry soil)	Mean CO_2 production rate for replicates (mg CO_2/day/kg dry soil)

Interpretation of the Results

1. Describe the general results of the soda lime experiments. What did you learn about CO$_2$ production rates in your samples?

2. Were CO$_2$ production levels higher or lower than you expected for each type of sample or treatment? Explain.

3. If you had replicates of the same type of soil or compost, did you see much variability between these replicates? Explain what you think caused any variability that you found.

4. If you measured CO_2 in different treatments (e.g., presence or absence of worms), explain your results. Which treatment had higher levels of CO_2 production? What are some possible reasons for the differences?

5. If you had a chance to do a follow-up experiment, what would you do differently based on what you have learned? For example, can you think of other treatments that would be useful to investigate?

6. Why is it useful to measure decomposition rates in soil or compost?

PROTOCOL 9. MEASURING DISSOLVED CARBON DIOXIDE

Objective

To measure carbon dioxide concentrations in water.

Background

Through the process of respiration, plants, animals, and microorganisms break down organic compounds to obtain the energy needed to sustain life. Carbon dioxide (CO_2) is produced as a waste product.

Respiration:

organic matter + oxygen → carbon dioxide + water + energy

In aquatic systems, the dissolved CO_2 concentration can be used as an indicator of the rate of respiration vs. photosynthesis. Plants produce CO_2 as a waste product of respiration, but they also use CO_2 to build food through the process of photosynthesis. While respiration occurs 24 hours per day, photosynthesis occurs only in the light. Ponds that are rich in plant life therefore have swings in CO_2 concentration over the course of the day and night.

Bacteria and fungi produce CO_2 when they break down organic wastes. In water containing a lot of organic matter, microbes grow and reproduce rapidly. As a result, they use up a lot of oxygen and produce high CO_2 concentrations. Fish tend to avoid water with CO_2 concentrations of 1–6 mg/L, and higher concentrations can kill them.

This protocol measures CO_2 concentrations in water, based on the same chemical reactions used in packaged test kits (such as LaMotte #7297-DR or Hach #143601). If the sample contains CO_2, it is acidic. As you add drops of NaOH, this base neutralizes the acid according to the following chemical reaction:

$$CO_2 \quad + \quad NaOH \quad → \quad NaHCO_3$$
carbon dioxide   *sodium hydroxide*   *sodium bicarbonate*

You stop adding NaOH when the solution turns pink, which occurs at a pH of 8.3.

Materials (per student group)

▶ 50 mL buret or "Poor Man's Buret" (e.g., Flinn #AP8752)

▶ Ring stand with buret clamp

▶ 100 mL flask or beaker

▶ 50 mL water sample

▶ 2 drops phenolphthalein indicator solution (1%)

▶ 50 mL 0.02 N NaOH solution

▶ Goggles

▶ Gloves

NOTE: Samples should be analyzed promptly after collection because the concentration of dissolved CO_2 is likely to change over time. If you will be collecting samples in the field for analysis in the lab, fill the sample bottles completely (leaving no room for air), keep them on ice, and perform the lab analyses as soon as possible after sampling.

Procedure

1. Wearing goggles and gloves, attach the buret to the ring stand so that it is suspended over the beaker or flask. Fill the buret with 50 mL NaOH solution.

2. Gently pour 50 mL of your sample into the beaker or flask, being careful not to shake the sample or to create bubbles.

3. If your lab table is a dark color, place a piece of white paper under the beaker so that you will be able to see color change in the solution.

4. Add two drops phenolphthalein indicator solution. If a pink or red color develops, there is no dissolved carbon dioxide. If no color develops, go on to the next step.

5. One drop at a time, add NaOH solution and gently swirl the sample. Continue until a light pink color develops and does not disappear when swirled.

6. Read on the buret how many mL of NaOH solution have been used.

Analysis

Use the following equation to calculate the CO_2 concentration in your solution:

CO_2 concentration = _____ mL NaOH x 17.6 = _____ mg CO_2/L

(17.6 converts from mL NaOH to mg CO_2/L. In case you're interested in the math, here's how it is derived):

$$\frac{mL\ NaOH}{50\ mL\ sample} \times \frac{0.02\ mol\ NaOH}{L} \times \frac{1\ mol\ CO_2}{mol\ NaOH} \times \frac{44\ g\ CO_2}{mol} \times \frac{1000\ mg}{g} = mg\ CO_2/L$$

The final step is to interpret these results. Your interpretations will depend on your particular experiment. How do your data compare with the predictions you made at the beginning of your experiment?

   If you tested water from a lake or stream, keep in mind that fish and other aquatic organisms tend to avoid water with CO_2 concentrations of 1–6 mg/L, and higher concentrations can kill them. In waters with high CO_2 concentrations, the dissolved oxygen concentrations tend to be low. How would you explain this correlation?

PROTOCOL 10. MEASURING DISSOLVED OXYGEN

Objective

To measure the concentration of dissolved oxygen in a water sample.

Background

Dissolved oxygen (DO) is a critical factor determining the water quality in streams, lakes, and other water bodies. DO concentrations depend on a combination of physical and chemical factors such as temperature, salinity, and the degree of mixing of water and air (e.g., through turbulent stream flow). They also depend on the biological processes of photosynthesis and respiration, which have opposite effects on DO concentrations. Oxygen gets released into water as a by-product of photosynthesis by algae and aquatic plants:

> ### Photosynthesis:
>
> **carbon dioxide + water + solar energy →organic matter + oxygen**

However, through cellular respiration, aquatic organisms continuously use dissolved oxygen in the process of breaking down organic compounds to obtain the energy needed to sustain life:

> ### Respiration:
>
> **organic matter + oxygen →carbon dioxide + water + energy**

Although respiration occurs throughout the day and night, photosynthesis occurs only in daylight hours. Water bodies that are rich in plant life therefore experience swings in dissolved concentration over the course of 24 hours. Low DO levels also can be caused by input of excess organic matter such as inadequately treated sewage. As decomposer microbes work to break down these wastes, they use oxygen.

Most fish and other aquatic organisms cannot survive DO concentrations lower than 2 mg/L, and concentrations of 5 mg/L or above generally are required to sustain healthy populations. Young fish, fish eggs, and aquatic invertebrates are particularly sensitive to DO levels. Highly sensitive fish such as salmon and trout, and invertebrates such as stonefly nymphs, may require DO concentrations of 7 mg/L or higher, whereas more tolerant species such as catfish and sludge worms can survive in waters with lower DO concentrations.

This protocol uses a technique called the Winkler-Azide titration, based on the same chemical reactions used in packaged test kits (e.g., Flinn #FB1113 or AB1154, or Hach #2351400) to measure dissolved oxygen in a water sample.

Materials (per water sample)

- Scale with 1 g accuracy
- 50 mL buret or "Poor Man's Buret" (e.g., Flinn #AP8752)
- Ring stand with buret clamp
- 500 mL Erlenmeyer flask
- 100 mL graduated cylinder

▶ 3 1-mL pipettes

▶ Pipette bulb or pump

▶ 1 mL manganous sulfate solution*

▶ 1 mL alkaline potassium iodide azide solution*

▶ 50 mL sodium thiosulfate solution, 0.025 N*

▶ 0.5 mL starch indicator solution*

▶ 5 g sulfamic acid powder

▶ 300 mL BOD bottle per sample (e.g., Wards #17W0570)**

▶ Water sample to completely fill the BOD bottle

▶ Goggles

▶ Gloves

Procedure

> **NOTE:** The concentration of dissolved oxygen in a water sample will change if the sample warms up, gets shaken, or does not get analyzed shortly after sampling. If you need to store your samples before analysis, first proceed through Part 2 below in order to "fix" the sample so that the oxygen concentrations will not change during storage.

Part 1. Taking a sample

Rinse the BOD bottle several times. Submerge the bottle, remove the cap, and allow the bottle to fill. Tap the bottle to dislodge any air bubbles. Put the cap in place while the bottle is still under water. The cap has a cone-shaped piece inside it that is designed to force bubbles out. If any bubbles are trapped in your bottle, empty and refill until you get a bubble-free sample.

If you cannot submerge your bottle, another possibility is to use a siphon. It is important to minimize bubbling or mixing with the water and air because you don't want to introduce additional oxygen into the sample.

Once you have collected one or more samples, proceed immediately to Part 2 to "fix" the dissolved oxygen.

Part 2. Fixing the sample (Carry out these steps immediately after collecting your sample.)

In this series of steps, the dissolved oxygen in your sample gets chemically bound so that it will not continue to change over time.

---

*Preparation of these solutions is described in the *Teacher Edition*.

**BOD stands for biological oxygen demand (see Protocol 11). BOD bottles are designed to be airtight and to be able to be filled to overflowing so that no air bubbles get trapped. If you do not have BOD bottles, you could try using flasks or bottles with tightly fitting corks, but be careful not to entrap bubbles. Smaller (60 mL) BOD bottles that come with test kits (e.g., LaMotte #0688-DO) work fine, but you will need to adjust the amounts of reagents used for the smaller sample size.

1. Wearing goggles and gloves, use a 1 mL pipette to gently add 1 mL of manganous sulfate solution to your sample. Use another 1 mL pipette to add 1 mL of alkaline potassium iodide azide solution. It is OK if your sample overflows a bit when you add these reagents.

2. Cap the bottle and gently invert 5–10 times to mix. A cloudy precipitate will form. Allow the bottle to sit undisturbed for several minutes until the cloudiness has settled below the shoulder of the bottle.

3. Add 5 g sulfamic acid powder. Cap the bottle with no bubbles, and gently shake until the acid crystals and the cloudy precipitate have dissolved. The solution should now be clear yellow to yellow-brown. The darker the color, the higher the DO concentration.

At this point, your sample is chemically "fixed," meaning that the oxygen has been chemically modified to a form that won't change when exposed to the air. You can continue on to Part 3 immediately, or refrigerate your fixed samples for analysis within eight hours.

Part 3. Measuring dissolved oxygen

In the final series of steps, you perform a titration, gradually adding one solution to another until the desired endpoint is reached. In this case, you detect the endpoint using color change in the sample solution.

1. Wearing goggles and gloves, fill the buret with sodium thiosulfate solution to the top line.

2. Using a 100 mL graduated cylinder, carefully measure 200 mL of your sample into a 500 mL Erlenmeyer flask.

3. If you are working on a dark colored lab bench, put a piece of white paper under your flask so that you will be able to observe the color of the solution. If the sample solution is a pale shade of yellow, skip to Step 5.

4. From the buret, add sodium thiosulfate solution drop by drop to the sample in the flask, gently swirling the flask between additions. Continue until the sample turns a pale straw color. The exact shade of yellow is not important. The point is to stop before the solution becomes colorless because the starch indicator solution you will add in Step 5 will make this endpoint easier to detect.

5. Using another 1 mL pipette, add 0.5 mL starch indicator solution to the sample solution in your flask, which should cause the solution to become blue or purple.

6. Continue adding sodium thiosulfate solution one drop at a time from the buret, gently swirling the flask after each addition and watching for color changes. The blue should become lighter as you add more sodium thiosulfate solution, until finally the sample becomes colorless. When you get close to the endpoint, the solution may become clear at the surface but then change back to light blue when swirled. Add another drop and try again until the entire solution is colorless after mixing.

7. On the buret, read the volume of sodium thiosulfate solution that you used in the titration. This converts directly into the DO concentration in your water sample:

Sodium Thiosulfate volume (mL) = Dissolved Oxygen (mg/L)

Analysis

Your presentation and interpretation of your results will depend on your initial goal in deciding to measure dissolved oxygen. For example, if you are carrying out experiments on decomposition, then your goal may be to look at changes in DO over time as biodegradation occurs, or perhaps to compare trends in DO and carbon dioxide concentrations.

Another possibility is that your goal was to compare DO concentrations in a lake or pond at various times of night and day. In this case, you might choose to make a graph showing how DO varies over time. You also could compare your DO measurements to the levels required by fish and other aquatic organisms (see the Background section in this protocol).

If other students have measured DO using samples taken at the same time and place as your own, you could take a look at the variability among samples. Another possibility is to compare measurement techniques, such as using an electronic probe vs. carrying out the Protocol 10 titration. Although electronic probes are much quicker and easier to use than the titration method, sometimes the results can be misleading. The digital read-outs seem precise, but the numbers will be meaningless unless the probe has been properly maintained and calibrated.

PROTOCOL 11. MEASURING BIOCHEMICAL OXYGEN DEMAND (BOD)

Objective

To measure the amount of oxygen used to break down organic matter and chemicals in water over a period of five days.

Background

If you measure dissolved oxygen in a water sample, you determine the concentration at that particular moment. However, dissolved oxygen levels do not remain constant in lakes and streams. As aquatic plants carry out photosynthesis, they add oxygen to the water. Oxygen from the atmosphere gets added to streams as the water tumbles over rocks and mixes with air. Dissolved oxygen levels also can drop, sometimes to levels that are dangerously low for aquatic life. This happens when the water contains too much organic matter because microorganisms use oxygen in the process of decay.

Biochemical oxygen demand (BOD) measures how much dissolved oxygen gets used in a water sample over a period of five days. This is an important measurement at wastewater treatment facilities because it indicates whether the level of organic matter in the sewage has been sufficiently reduced. If wastewater that is high in organic matter (and therefore has a high BOD) is released into a lake or stream, it is likely to cause ecological problems because dissolved oxygen levels will drop too low to support sensitive species. One of the goals of wastewater treatment is to lower BOD to acceptable levels before the treated wastewater gets released.

In unpolluted lakes and streams, the BOD usually is less than 5 mg/L. Nutrient-rich ponds and wetlands are likely to have BOD values ranging up to 10 mg/L. Raw sewage can have BOD levels up to 300 mg/L. Each wastewater treatment plant has a discharge permit that specifies the allowable BOD level for treated wastewater, and generally this ranges between 8 and 150 mg/L BOD, depending on site-specific conditions such as the size and condition of the receiving water body.

Materials (per sample)

▶ Incubator set at 20°C (optional)

▶ Materials listed in Protocol 10, or a dissolved oxygen test kit (e.g., Flinn # FB1113) or probe

▶ 2 BOD bottles* (only 1 is needed if you will be using a probe)

▶ Foil, paper, or tape to exclude light from 1 BOD bottle

▶ Water sample (at least enough to fill your BOD bottles)

▶ Goggles

▶ Gloves

---

*BOD bottles are designed to be airtight and to be able to be filled to overflowing so that no air bubbles get trapped. If you do not have BOD bottles, you could try using flasks or bottles with tightly fitting corks, but be careful not to entrap air bubbles. Smaller (60 mL) BOD bottles that come with test kits (e.g., LaMotte #0688-DO) provide a less expensive alternative to the standard 300 mL BOD bottles.

Procedure

> **NOTE:** To keep it simple, these directions are written for a single sample. If you have replicates or will be testing more than one sample, you will need to increase the numbers of bottles accordingly. Be sure to wear goggles and gloves.

1. *If you will be measuring DO with Protocol 10 or a test kit:*

   a. Fill two BOD bottles by lowering them gently into the water and allowing them to fill slowly without mixing in bubbles. Cap both bottles, making sure not to trap air at the top.

   b. Immediately measure and record the dissolved oxygen in one of the two bottles. This is your Day #1 reading.

   If you will be measuring DO with an electronic probe:

   a. Use the probe to take an initial DO reading from the water you want to test for BOD.

   b. Fill one BOD bottle by lowering it gently into the water and allowing it to fill slowly without mixing in bubbles. Cap the bottle, making sure not to trap air at the top.

2. Whichever way you performed Step 1, at this point you should have one BOD bottle filled with the sample you wish to test. Wrap this bottle in foil, paper, or other material to provide complete darkness during incubation. (Excluding light prevents photosynthesis, which would affect your DO reading.)

3. Incubate in the dark for five days at 20°C. This is close to room temperature, so if you do not have an incubator, place the bottles in a dark drawer or closet where the temperature will remain relatively even. During the five-day incubation period, no oxygen should be able to enter or leave the solution because the bottle is filled to the brim and tightly sealed.

4. After five days, remove the sample from the incubator and measure the DO concentration using a test kit or probe. This is your Day #5 reading.

Analysis

1. Calculate the BOD by subtracting the dissolved oxygen concentration on Day #5 from the concentration you measured on Day #1:

Day #1 Dissolved Oxygen (mg/L)	–	Day #5 Dissolved Oxygen (mg/L)	=	Biochemical Oxygen Demand (mg/L)

In samples containing large amounts of organic matter, it is possible that your final dissolved oxygen reading will be 0 mg/L, indicating that all available dissolved oxygen has been used up during the five-day incubation period. To get an accurate BOD reading, you would need to take a new sample, dilute it, and run the test again. If you dilute by a factor of 10, then you would multiply the result by 10 in order to convert to a BOD score for the undiluted sample.

2. The final step is to interpret your BOD results. Remember, BOD is a measure of the amount of oxygen needed to decompose the organic material and chemicals in your sample. For comparison with typical BOD values in natural waters and in treated or untreated sewage, see the Background section of this protocol. Consider these questions:

a. How does the BOD of your sample compare with an unpolluted stream or to the range of values that are allowed for treated wastewater?

b. If you have analyzed replicates of the same water sample, how close are the BOD values for these replicates? What are some possible sources of this variation? (What would you expect might not be identical from one bottle to the next?)

c. If you have analyzed several types of samples, how do their BOD values compare? Do they vary in the way that you expected when you set up the experiment?

d. Discuss your results and what you think they mean in terms of water quality.

COMPOSTING AND LANDFILLING

PROTOCOL 12. USING SODA BOTTLE BIOREACTORS FOR BIODEGRADATION EXPERIMENTS

PROTOCOL 12A. BUILDING SODA BOTTLE BIOREACTORS

Objective

To design and build bioreactors for indoor composting and landfill experiments.

Background

When you think of composting, chances are you think of outdoor bins or piles. But composting can also be carried out right in the classroom, using containers ranging in size from soda bottles to garbage cans. Called *bioreactors*, these systems are too small to handle large quantities of organic wastes. However, they are ideal for conducting research into the conditions needed for biodegradation processes to occur. Depending on how you set up your bioreactors, they can simulate the conditions in either a composting system or a landfill.

The instructions below provide a starting point for building classroom bioreactors, but many variations are possible. Feel free to make adaptations using whatever materials you have available or ideas you have about better design possibilities. As you design your bioreactors, think about what experiments you would like to carry out in them because this may affect your design decisions (see pp. 101–108 in Section 3 for some ideas about possible research topics). Think about how many bioreactors you will need and what characteristics will be needed for the experiments you have in mind.

Materials (per bioreactor)

▶ 2 2-liter or 3-liter soda bottles

▶ Styrofoam plate or tray

▶ 1 small plastic container such as a margarine tub that fits inside the bottom of the soda bottle (optional—see Step 3 below)

▶ Drill or nail for making holes

▶ Duct tape or clear packaging tape

▶ Utility knife or sharp-pointed scissors

▶ Fine-meshed screen or fabric (such as a piece of nylon stocking) large enough to cover holes at top and bottom of soda bottle, to keep flies out (optional)

▶ Dial thermometer with stem at least 20 cm long (e.g., Ward's #15 V 0890), for composting experiments

Procedure

Although these instructions call for building a single bioreactor, you may decide to build several so that you will be able to test various bioreactor designs or various mixtures of compost ingredients. Or you might decide to keep the design and ingredients constant and to make several replicate bioreactors so that you can test the variability within a single type of composting system. If you decide to build multiple bioreactors, you can use a single thermometer to monitor them all.

1. Using a utility knife or sharp-pointed scissors, cut the top off one soda bottle just below the shoulder and the other just above the shoulder (Figure 2.5). Use the top from Bottle 1 as a cover for the bottom of Bottle 2. It will fit snugly with a slight overlap (Figure 2.6). Once the bioreactor is completed and filled, you will tape this cover into place.

2. The next step is to make a Styrofoam circle that fits snugly inside the soda bottle. This will form a tray that holds up the compost ingredients, providing space below for air circulation and drainage. Trace a circle the diameter of the soda bottle on a Styrofoam plate and cut it out. Use a nail to punch holes through the Styrofoam tray for aeration and drainage.

3. If your soda bottle is indented at the bottom, the indentations may provide sufficient support for the Styrofoam tray. Otherwise, you will need to fashion a support. For example, you could wire or tape the tray in place. Another possibility for holding up the tray is to support it on a small plastic container, placed upside down in the bottom of the soda bottle. If you choose this technique, you may need to drill holes in this container so that it doesn't block drainage and air circulation through the tray.

4. Fit the Styrofoam tray into the soda bottle, roughly 4–5 cm from the bottom. Below this tray, make air holes in the sides of the soda bottle. This can be done with a drill or by carefully heating a nail and using it to melt holes through the plastic. The object is to make sure that air will be able to enter the bioreactor, diffuse through the compost, and exit through the holes or tubing at the top. Avoid making holes in the very bottom of the bottle unless you plan to use a pan underneath to collect whatever liquids will drain out.

5. Make final adjustments based on how you plan to use your bioreactor. For example, if you plan to investigate the effects of aeration on biodegradation, you might want to block the air holes in one bioreactor and not in another.

6. If you plan to make compost, Protocol 12b gives additional guidance for designing and filling your bioreactor.

FIGURE 2.5
Making a Soda Bottle Bioreactor: Cut Bottles at Two Different Heights

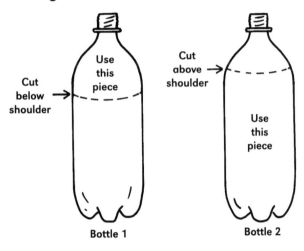

Cut below shoulder → Use this piece

Cut above shoulder →

Use this piece

Bottle 1   Bottle 2

FIGURE 2.6
Making a Soda Bottle Bioreactor: Fit Together the Two Pieces

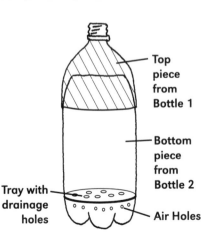

Top piece from Bottle 1

Bottom piece from Bottle 2

Tray with drainage holes

Air Holes

PROTOCOL 12B. COMPOSTING IN SODA BOTTLE BIOREACTORS

Objective

To create compost in soda bottle bioreactors.

FIGURE 2.7
Filled Soda Bottle
Bioreactor

Background

It's quite simple to use bioreactors to investigate biodegradation that occurs at room temperature. You simply fill the container with soil and whatever wastes you choose to investigate, and decide how you wish to regulate environmental factors such as temperature, light, and moisture. (See Figure 2.7 for a filled bioreactor.)

However, it also is possible to use soda bottle bioreactors to make compost that heats up due to rapid growth and respiration of decomposer microbes. Because bioreactors are so small, it is trickier than in a large outdoor compost pile to get the right combination of ingredients and environmental conditions that enable the compost to get hot. The following guidelines will help get you started in providing these conditions so that you can carry out experiments related to heat-producing compost.

Materials

▶ Bioreactor built in Protocol 12a

▶ Chopped vegetable scraps such as lettuce leaves, carrot or potato peelings, and apple cores, or chopped yard wastes such as weeds or grass clippings

▶ Bulking agent such as wood shavings or 1 cm pieces of paper egg cartons, cardboard, or wood

▶ Insulation materials that will fit around the bioreactor

▶ Flexible tubing to provide ventilation out the top (optional—see Step 6 below)

Procedure

1. Determine what kinds of materials you want to compost. A variety of ingredients will work, but in general you will want a mixture that includes some materials that are high in carbon and others that are high in nitrogen.

   All plant materials contain both carbon and nitrogen, but in different relative amounts. Brown, dry materials such as wood shavings, shredded newspaper, and brown leaves are relatively high in carbon and low in nitrogen. Colorful, moist materials such as food scraps or fresh grass clippings are the opposite—low in carbon but high in nitrogen. Avoid meat or dairy products. Chopped up apple cores, banana peels, melon rinds, salad trimmings, potato peelings, and garden weeds are examples of high-nitrogen wastes you can use in soda bottle composting.

   By mixing roughly equal amounts of materials from the high-carbon and high-nitrogen groups, you can achieve a successful mixture that will get hot when composted. However, there are a couple other considerations to keep in mind:

   ▶ *Moisture:* Your initial mixture should be about as moist as a wrung-out sponge. If it is too dry, just mix in some water. If it is too wet, drain the mixture and make sure that it includes enough dry, brown materials.

   ▶ *Particle size:* In soda bottle bioreactors, particles need to be smaller than in larger composting systems. In soda bottles, composting will proceed best if the materials are no larger than 1–2 cm in size.

2. Loosely fill your bioreactor. Remember that you want air to be able to work its way through the pores in the compost, so keep your mix light and fluffy and do not pack it down.

3. Put the top piece of the bioreactor in place and attach it with tape.

4. Cover the top hole with a piece of screen or nylon stocking held in place with a rubber band. Alternatively, if you are worried about potential odors, you can ventilate your bioreactor by running rubber tubing out the top. In this case, drill a hole through the screw-on soda bottle lid, insert tubing through the hole, and lead the tubing out the window or into a ventilation hood.

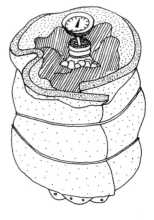

FIGURE 2.8
Insulated Soda
Bottle Bioreactor

5. To prevent problems with flies, it is a good idea to cover all air holes with pieces of nylon stocking or other fine-meshed fabric.

6. Because soda bottle bioreactors are much smaller than a compost pile, they will need to be insulated to retain the heat that is generated during decomposition (Figure 2.8). You can experiment with various types and amounts of insulation, making sure not to block the ventilation holes.

7. Now you are ready to watch the composting process at work! You can chart the progress of your compost by taking temperature readings. Insert a thermometer down into the compost through the top of the soda bottle. For the first few days, the temperature readings should be taken at least daily, or more often if possible.

In these small bioreactors, it is possible that temperatures will reach their peak in less than 24 hours. To avoid missing a possible early peak, use a max/min thermometer or a continuously recording temperature sensor, or be sure to measure the temperatures several hours after start-up, then again the next morning. Continue taking temperature readings until the compost has returned to room temperature.

Analysis

Make a graph of the temperature of your compost over time. Soda bottle bioreactors generally reach temperatures of 40–45°C, somewhat lower than temperatures achieved in larger composting systems. If conditions are not right, no noticeable heating will occur. This may be due to any one of the various factors that affect microbial growth and decomposition—C:N ratios, moisture levels, air flow, or insulation.

Describe changes in appearance of your compost ingredients over time. Because soda bottle bioreactors are so small, you may not end up with a product that looks as finished as the compost from larger systems. However, within a few weeks you should find that the volume shrinks by one-half to two-thirds and that the original materials are no longer recognizable. You can let the compost age in the soda bottles for several months, or transfer it to other containers or outdoor piles to continue the breakdown process.

Think of experiments you could conduct using soda bottle bioreactors. For example, you could build several bioreactors and investigate how various design decisions or mixtures of ingredients affect the temperature profile during the composting process. Additional ideas are discussed in Section 3, pp. 104–105. If you are analyzing the results of an experiment you have already conducted, think about what you have learned from your results and what you can conclude about further experiments that would be interesting to try next.*

---

*For more information about composting experiments, see *Composting in the Classroom: Scientific Inquiry for High School Students,* by N. M. Trautmann and M. E. Krasny. 1998. (Dubuque, IA: Kendall/Hunt. ISBN 0-7872-4433-3.)

BIOREMEDIATION

PROTOCOL 13. GROWING ENRICHMENT CULTURES

Objective
To grow a culture of microorganisms that can degrade motor oil.

Background
Through bioremediation, we can increase the rate at which microorganisms break down environmental pollutants. In Protocol 13, we will be using motor oil as an example pollutant, but you can adapt these protocols for investigation of other pollutants of your choice.

The crash of an oil tanker creates an ecological disaster and big headlines in the news. However, you may be surprised to learn that much of the oil that ends up in lakes and oceans comes from much smaller leaks and spills. One significant source is people who change the motor oil in their own vehicles, then pour the used oil on the ground or into a storm drain rather than recycling it or disposing of it safely. Another source is leakage or spills of oil from vehicles in parking lots and on roads. Runoff draining from these surfaces carries oil into streams or other surface waters.

An *enrichment culture* is a culture of microorganisms that can grow in the presence of a chemical pollutant. In this case, our contaminant is motor oil. The enrichment culture contains these ingredients:

▶ a source of bacteria, such as soil or compost,

▶ a nutrient solution that buffers the culture at a pH of 7 and provides all needed nutrients except carbon, and

▶ motor oil or some other chemical pollutant, which serves as the carbon source.

In this protocol, we will be growing an enrichment culture of microbes in a solution containing nitrogen, phosphorus, calcium, magnesium, sulfur, and iron—all of the major nutrients needed for growth except carbon. Motor oil will be the only source of carbon provided. Therefore, the microbes that grow well in this solution will be the ones that can "eat" oil, using it as their carbon source.

Materials (per student group)
▶ Metric balance with 1 g accuracy

▶ Incubator

▶ Bunsen burners

▶ Matches or striker

▶ Disinfectant solution such as a household cleaning solution

▶ 1 g fresh sample of soil or compost

▶ <1 mL of each of the following stock nutrient solutions* (sterile):

$CaCl_2 \cdot 2H_2O$ $FeCl_3 \cdot 6H_2O$

$(NH_4)_2HPO_4$ K_2HPO_4

$MgSO_4 \cdot 7H_2O$

---

*The *Teacher Edition* includes instructions for making the stock nutrient solutions, maintaining sterile conditions, and disposing of microbiological cultures when you are finished with them.

- ❯ 2 250-mL flasks, each containing 100 mL distilled water (sterile)

- ❯ 2 1-mL pipettes (sterile)

- ❯ 5 0.1-mL pipettes (sterile)

- ❯ Pipette bulb or pump

- ❯ Glass marker or tape for labels

- ❯ Scoopula

- ❯ Goggles

- ❯ Gloves

Procedure

1. Wearing goggles and gloves, wipe down your work area with disinfectant solution.

2. Using sterile procedures and a separate pipette for each solution, add the following quantities of nutrient solutions to the sterilized distilled water in each of your flasks:

Sterile Nutrient Solution	Amount (mL)
$CaCl_2 \cdot 2H_2O$	0.1
$(NH_4)_2HPO_4$	0.1
$MgSO_4 \cdot 7H_2O$	0.1
$FeCl_3 \cdot 6H_2O$	0.1
K_2HPO_4	0.8

3. Using scoopula, add 1 g soil or compost to each flask. This is your source of microorganisms.

4. Label one flask "0.01 mL Motor Oil" and the other "0.1 mL Motor Oil," then add the appropriate amounts of oil to each flask. (If you are using contaminants other than motor oil, you will have to decide on appropriate contaminant concentrations. The goal is to provide the contaminant compound in a concentration that will support growth of a bacterial population. If the concentration is too high, it will kill the microbes. On the other hand, a concentration that is too low will not supply enough carbon to sustain bacterial growth. It therefore is a good idea to start with a wide range of concentrations in order to determine the concentration that will yield the best growth.)

5. Incubate at 30°C for one week. Swirl the flasks at least once each day to mix and aerate. By the end of the week, your flasks should contain cultures of microbes that have grown using motor oil as their source of carbon.

PROTOCOL 14. ISOLATING THE DEGRADERS

Objective

To isolate types of bacteria that can "eat" motor oil, using it as their carbon source.

Background

In Protocol 13, you grew liquid cultures of microorganisms capable of degrading motor oil. Now you will take samples of the cultures and plate them out on agar in petri dishes. This will enable you to look for evidence of digestion of motor oil by individual bacterial colonies that grow on the agar.

Materials (per student group)

⬤ Incubator (optional)

⬤ Dissecting microscope or overhead projector (for viewing cultures)

⬤ Bunsen burner

⬤ Matches or striker

⬤ Disinfectant solution such as a household cleaning solution

⬤ Enrichment culture (from Protocol 13)

⬤ Glass marker or tape for labels

⬤ Scoopula

⬤ Bacteriological spreading rod or cotton swab (sterile)

⬤ 3 petri dishes containing no-carbon agar* (sterile; at least 1 dish for the 0.01 mL motor oil culture, 1 for the 0.1 mL motor oil culture, and 1 for the control, but it is better to have replicates if possible)

⬤ Goggles

⬤ Gloves

Procedure

1. Wearing goggles and gloves, wipe down your work area with disinfectant solution.

2. Label your petri dishes with your name, the date, and the type of sample: "0.01 mL Motor Oil," "0.1 mL Motor Oil," and "Control."

3. Put a few drops of motor oil into a flat dish (an extra petri lid works well). Dip a sterile spreading rod into this motor oil, then spread the oil as uniformly as possible in a thin layer over the surface of the agar in each of the labeled petri dishes. You should see a thin black layer when you view the samples under the dissecting microscope.

4. Using sterile techniques, incubate the labeled petri dishes with the appropriate culture solutions. Do this by placing 0.01 mL drops in three different sections of each dish, then use a sterile spreading rod to spread each drop into a small circle about the size of a dime.

---

*The *Teacher Edition* includes instructions for making the no-carbon agar, maintaining sterile conditions, and disposing of microbiological cultures when you are finished with them.

5. In the "Control" dishes, repeat Step 4 using drops of sterile distilled water in place of your enrichment cultures.

6. Place the petri dishes upside down in an incubator at 30°C and leave them there for 24 hours.

Analysis

1. After the 24-hour incubation period, examine your cultures using a dissecting microscope or overhead projector. Are any colonies growing in the control dishes? Is this what you expected? If not, how might you explain the results?

2. In the dishes that you inoculated with your enrichment cultures, observe the colonies and record their characteristics. Look for evidence of digestion of the motor oil—are there areas with no oil surrounding one or more of the colonies? Make a sketch showing what you have found.

Example sketch:

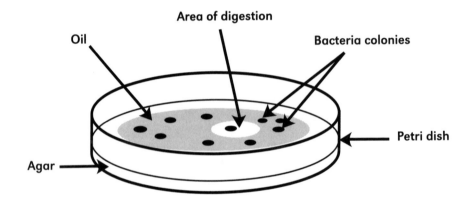

3. What can you conclude about the bacteria you have grown? Are they capable of degrading motor oil? When making conclusions about the oil-eating capabilities of microbes in your soil samples, it is important to recognize that only a tiny fraction of the bacterial strains found in nature can be cultured successfully under laboratory conditions.

4. See pp. 106–108 in Section 3 for ideas about experiments you could carry out using these cultures to investigate various aspects of bioremediation.

PROTOCOL PLANNING AND REVIEW FORMS

See Table 3 (p. 11) in the *Teacher Edition* for a description of where each of these forms fits in the Environmental Inquiry research process.

Additional forms are included in Protocol 8 for data analysis (pp. 69–76).

PROTOCOL PLANNING FORM

Name _____ Date _____

1. What is the name of the protocol you will be using?

2. What is the purpose of this protocol?

   ❏ To monitor existing conditions

   ❏ To compare conditions in two or more different habitats or ecosystems

   ❏ To perform an experiment in the laboratory

   ❏ To perform an experiment in the field

   ❏ Other. Describe:

3. What question are you hoping to answer using this protocol?

4. What type of samples will you be using?

5. Describe the field sites or lab setup you will be using:

DATA ANALYSIS PEER REVIEW FORM

Name _____ Date _____

Are the data presented clearly?

Very clear	❏	Comments about what was done well:
Mostly clear	❏	
Somewhat clear	❏	Suggestions for improvement:
Largely unclear	❏	

Are the conclusions clearly stated?

Very clear	❏	Comments about what was done well:
Mostly clear	❏	
Somewhat clear	❏	Suggestions for improvement:
Largely unclear	❏	

Do the data clearly support the conclusions?

Very clear	❏	Comments about what was done well:
Mostly clear	❏	
Somewhat clear	❏	Suggestions for improvement:
Largely unclear	❏	

INTERACTIVE RESEARCH:
EXPERIMENTS AND FIELD STUDIES

IDEAS FOR BIODEGRADATION RESEARCH

INVERTEBRATE LIFE

Once you have mastered one or more invertebrate collection techniques, you can carry out research projects on a wide range of topics.

Compost Invertebrates

If you have access to an outdoor compost pile, it would be interesting to monitor invertebrate life over the course of the composting process. For example, you could sample for invertebrates once a week for several months, and compare the types and abundance of organisms that you find during that time.

Some compost piles heat up. This is caused by rapid growth and respiration of microorganisms as they break down the available organic matter. If your compost gets hot, you could investigate what happens to invertebrates during this process. Do they disappear while the compost is hot, or do they move to the cooler edges of the pile? What happens to their populations as the temperature in the pile becomes cooler?

What happens when you mix compost into a garden or use it as mulch around outdoor plants—does this have any effect on invertebrate populations in these areas? You could compare similar sites, with and without addition of compost. Or you could compare a single site over time, before and after treatment with compost.

Soil Invertebrates

What role do invertebrates play in the decomposition of leaves on a forest floor? Do you think that bacteria and fungi can accomplish this task alone, or do worms, beetles, and other invertebrates also play an important role? One way of investigating this question is to place a few leaves into mesh bags, bury them or place them on the ground surface, and observe what happens over the course of the next few months. If the bags have various mesh sizes, you could investigate the impacts of various sizes of decomposer organisms. For example, you could make bags with a very small mesh size using nylon stockings, a medium mesh size using mosquito netting or window screening, and a large mesh size using the bags in which onions or citrus fruits are sold.

Another possible research topic is to compare the types of invertebrates you can find in various types of soils and locations. For example, you could take samples from agricultural fields, home gardens, dirt roads, forests, and parks. Or you could take samples at various distances from the edge of a compost pile or garden, or compare plowed land with soil from a nearby pasture or lawn. In unplowed soils, you could look for differences in the abundance and types of organisms you find at various soil depths.

Where would you expect to find the greatest number or diversity of organisms? Why? What variables do you think are most important in determining where these organisms live? Can you think of an experiment that would help to determine whether these variables really do make a difference to invertebrate populations?

Aquatic Invertebrates

Stream invertebrates provide valuable clues about the quality of the water in which they live. Some species can live only in water with high dissolved oxygen concentrations, while others are more pollution-tolerant and can survive under low-oxygen conditions. By comparing the kinds and diversity of organisms you find at various sampling sites or dates, you can draw conclusions about the water quality. (This works only for rivers and streams; pond invertebrates cannot be used to evaluate water quality because they are adapted to living with low or fluctuating dissolved oxygen concentrations.)

Take a close look at individual organisms from streams and ponds. Can you figure out what adaptations they have for living in the environment in which you found them? Do they cling to rocks or burrow in the mud? Do they filter their food from the current, scrape algae off of rocks, or catch and eat live prey? Try sketching a possible food web for the organisms you have collected.

MICROBIAL LIFE

Using Protocols 6 and 7, you can compare microbe populations in various types of soil and compost, or from various stages in the composting process. Where would you expect to find the greatest number and assortment of microbes—in the top layers of soil just under the leaf litter in a forest, or deeper underground? How about in a garden versus in the middle of a dusty dirt road? What are the differences between these habitats, and how would you expect them to affect microbial life?

Think of experiments you could use to test which variables are most important in supporting a diverse and abundant population of microbes in soil or compost. Do changes in environmental conditions make a difference? Think about environmental factors such as moisture, temperature, and concentrations of nutrients or organic matter. Then you could plan an experiment to test the effects of one of these variables on microbial populations.

If you are making compost that heats up due to the rapid growth and respiration of decomposer microbes, you can use temperature readings to assess the rate at which biodegradation is occurring. For example, you could make a graph of temperature readings over time, then relate temperature to the types of microorganisms you find in the compost at each sampling event. The Bioremediation section (p. 106) has additional ideas about microbiology experiments.

CHEMICAL EFFECTS OF BIODEGRADATION

What conditions cause organic matter to break down quickly, and what slows down this process? What physical, chemical, and biological factors appear to be important? These kinds of questions are important when people design systems to decay wastes, such as compost systems and wastewater treatment plants.

Oxygen and Carbon Dioxide

Protocols 8 through 11 provide techniques for measuring the chemical effects of biodegradation on land or in water. Remember, biodegradation takes place when microorganisms use organic matter for food through the process of respiration:

> **organic matter + oxygen →carbon dioxide + water + energy**

Because this process uses oxygen and creates carbon dioxide, measurement of the concentration of these gases in water provides information about the rate at which biodegradation is occurring.

Think about the factors needed for biodegradation to take place:

▶ microorganisms,

▶ nutrients to support their growth, and

▶ favorable environmental conditions.

Table 3.1 lists some ideas about variables to consider in planning biodegradation experiments.

TABLE 3.1
Some Variables to Consider in Planning Biodegradation Experiments

Possible Sources of Microbes	Possible Sources of Nutrients	Environmental Factors
▶ Stream water or sediment ▶ Soil ▶ Compost	▶ Organic matter such as leaves or decaying plants ▶ Simple sugars such as sucrose ▶ Fertilizers or other nutrient solutions	▶ Temperature ▶ pH ▶ Aeration

What predictions can you make about the conditions under which biodegradation will occur? What chemical effects would you expect to see? Think about experiments that would enable you to test your predictions.

pH

Besides carbon dioxide and oxygen concentrations, another chemical measurement that can be useful in studying aquatic biodegradation is pH, a measure of acidity. To make predictions about pH changes in biodegradation experiments, you will need to know that the pH tends to go down as carbon dioxide gets absorbed in water and forms carbonic acid:

$$CO_2 + H_2O \rightarrow H_2CO_3$$

Would you expect pH to go up or down as aquatic biodegradation occurs? How might you test this prediction? One way is with an electronic pH probe. Another possibility is to use an indicator solution that changes color with pH change. For example, the universal indicator solution used in pH test kits is green at a neutral pH and changes through shades of yellow, orange, and red as the solution becomes more acidic. Bromthymol blue is another common pH indicator solution. At a pH of 7 or above, it is blue. As acid is added, it turns yellow. How might you use one of these indicator solutions to detect biodegradation in aquatic solutions?

COMPOSTING

If moist food scraps are placed in a container and left to sit for several weeks, the end product is likely to be a smelly mess that attracts flies. Given the proper conditions, these same food scraps can be composted to produce a material that looks and smells like rich earth and is prized by gardeners and farmers. What is the difference, and how can you avoid the smelly slop and produce instead a rich, earthy compost?

Bioreactor Design

How does the design of soda bottle bioreactors affect the temperature profile during composting? Does the quantity and type of insulation make a difference? Does it help to provide aeration?

Compost Ingredients

Garden supply stores and catalogs commonly sell compost "starters," which supposedly speed up the composting process. Develop a recipe for a compost starter and design a research project to test its effect on the compost temperature profile.

How well does human nutrition apply to compost microorganisms? For example, will the microbes get a "sugar high," demonstrated by a quick, high-temperature peak when sugary foods are available, compared with a longer but lower peak for more complex carbohydrates?

Some instructions call for adding lime (calcium or magnesium compounds ground into powder) to increase the pH when compost ingredients are mixed. Other instructions caution to avoid this because it causes a loss of nitrogen. How does adding various amounts of lime to the initial ingredients affect the pH of finished compost?

Microorganisms

Composting recipes sometimes call for inoculating the pile by mixing in a few handfuls of finished compost or garden soil. Is there any observable difference in appearance of microbes between composting systems that have and have not been inoculated?

Does the pH of the initial compost ingredients affect the types of microorganisms that appear during composting?

Compost Physics

What type of insulation works best for soda bottle bioreactors? Does it help to have a reflective layer? Do different types or amounts of insulation affect the temperature profile?

When constructing compost bins or piles, some people incorporate perforated pipe, wire mesh, or other systems to increase passive airflow. What is the effect of different methods of aeration on the temperature profile of any one compost system?

How do various techniques and schedules for turning a pile affect the temperature profile and the time needed for production of finished compost?

Try mixing the same ingredients in a large outdoor pile and a soda bottle bioreactor. Which system reaches hotter temperatures? Which remains hot longer? Why do you think this occurs? How does the temperature profile relate to the length of time it takes for the compost ingredients to break down into an unrecognizable form?

Effects of Compost on Plant Growth

The end product of composting is humus, the stable organic mixture that is left after the readily biodegradable materials have broken down. Humus is a valuable component of soils because it holds water and nutrients in the root zone where they are available to plants. Gardeners generally believe that the more compost they can add to their gardens, the better. Is this true—does addition of compost to garden soils help the plants to grow better? Is there any limit, or is "the more the better" a good guideline for gardeners? Can you think of experiments you could do to test these ideas?

If compost is applied in gardens before it is fully decomposed, the acids it contains can damage sensitive plants. (These acids get broken down as compost matures.) One way to test whether compost is ready for use is to test its rate of CO_2 production. Think about it— if the compost still contains readily available organic matter, the decomposer microbes will be growing rapidly. Through respiration, they will be producing CO_2. As the compost becomes mature, the food supply for decomposer microbes gets used up, so the rate at which CO_2 is produced goes down. Protocol 8 provides a way of measuring the rate at which CO_2 is released into the air. You can use this technique to compare the maturity of various compost samples. Then you can compare the compost maturity to its effects on sensitive plants such as tomato seedlings.

BIODEGRADATION IN LANDFILLS

About 55% of the 232 million tons of garbage produced in the U.S. each year gets sent to landfills (see Figure 1.7, p. 18). Much of this is biodegradable, but scientists who have sampled landfills have discovered that the rate of decay is extremely slow. Why do you think this is so? Think about the factors that determine how rapidly biodegradation will occur. If you wanted things to decay rapidly, what conditions do you think would be helpful?

▶ hot or cold?

▶ wet or dry?

▶ low or high oxygen levels?

▶ low or high availability of carbon, nitrogen, and other nutrients?

How do these conditions compare with what you are likely to find in a landfill? Remember, most landfills are not designed to promote biodegradation—instead, they are designed to contain wastes in a way that minimizes odors, pest problems, and contamination of groundwater or surface waters (see Chapter 2).

How do the conditions found in a typical landfill compare with optimal conditions for making compost? Think of experiments you could perform to test these ideas in soda bottle bioreactors (built in Protocol 12), or on an even smaller scale in petri dishes. Try making predictions about the rate at which food scraps will break down under various environmental conditions. Then test your predictions using simple experiments.

Before you start your experiments, make sure that you plan what end results to measure. For example, you might be able to measure differences in how much the food scraps decay over time. Or you can use rates of CO_2 production (Protocol 8) to compare the rates of biodegradation under various environmental conditions.

Biodegradable Plastics

Some disposable products are designed to be biodegradable, including certain types of plastic bags, fast food "clamshells," and disposable cups, plates, and eating utensils. Some of these products are designed to break down in compost, such as biodegradable plastic bags used for collection and disposal of leaves and yard wastes. Others are designed to break down when exposed to sunlight or rain so that plastic litter will decay rather than accumulating in the environment.

Try designing experiments to test whether biodegradable products truly are biodegradable, and under what conditions. Some fast food restaurants have begun using biodegradable packaging for hamburgers and other products. If you have access to such packaging, you could test whether it will fully decompose in a compost pile, or how long it would take to break down under the conditions you would expect to find in a landfill. How about under the conditions that litter would be exposed to along the edge of a highway? Think about how you might test whether biodegradable products are fully degrading—what would you expect the end products to be, and how might you measure them?

BIOREMEDIATION

Once you have learned how to grow enrichment cultures and to plate out colonies in petri dishes (Protocols 13 and 14), you can use these skills to conduct a wide range of experiments related to bioremediation and other topics in microbiology.

Cleaning Up an Oil Spill

When you grow cultures in a petri dish, you can select the colony that appears to be doing the best job of digesting the surrounding film of motor oil. As a next step, you could test the effectiveness of this microbe under more realistic oil spill conditions. For example, what happens in a liquid culture containing the basic nutrients listed in Protocol 13 and a small amount of motor oil as the carbon source? If you start with sterile conditions and then inoculate this culture with the one colony you have selected from your petri dish, then any degradation of oil that occurs should be the result of your selected type of microbe. What kinds of changes would you look for over time? What might you expect to see if you periodically look at samples under the microscope? What would be a good control for this experiment?

Using the liquid culture, you also could try changing one or more environmental factors in order to figure out how to enhance the growth of your selected organism. Is temperature important? Does it help to add more nitrogen? How about aerating the mixture as the culture grows? Think about the various factors that could be adjusted to promote the growth of this microbe in nature, then choose one or more to test in your laboratory solutions. Remember to change only one variable at a time and to provide a control for comparison with your experimental results.

Isolating the Degraders

One way to continue your bioremediation investigation would be to select the colony that appears to be doing the best job of digesting the motor oil in your petri dishes in Protocol 14, then grow a pure culture of just this type of microbe. To do this, you can use a sterile inoculating loop to pick up a single colony and transfer it to another sterile agar dish containing no-carbon agar and a thin film of motor oil. If you spread the microbes in an S shape on the agar, you will be able to look for this pattern once the colonies have grown (Figure 3.1). After 24 hours incubation, you should be able to see a collection of similar-looking colonies along the S curve that you drew. Colonies that don't look similar or that are not lined up on the curve provide an indication of contamination of your culture through nonsterile conditions.

FIGURE 3.1
S-Shape in Petri Dish

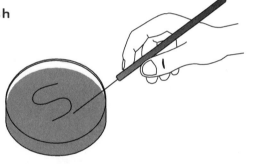

As a control, you could prepare a duplicate petri dish but leave it uninoculated. Can you think of other useful controls that would help you to check your experimental techniques or the biodegradation abilities of your selected organism?

If your goal is to find microbes that might be useful in cleaning up an oil spill, you will need to determine whether the microbes in your culture are capable of digesting motor oil. In petri dish cultures, you can check for a ring of digestion around each colony. In liquid solutions, you can look for signs that the oil is breaking down, but you will not be able to tell which particular organisms are responsible.

Comparing with Other Microbes

Another idea for continuing your bioremediation investigation would be to compare the oil-eating capabilities of microbes from various sources. Can you find oil-degraders wherever you look, or do they live only in specific locations? For example, are you more likely to find oil-eaters if you collect your sample from a parking lot than from the middle of a baseball field? Does it matter how much organic matter is present—does a culture grown from a sandy beach do as well as a culture grown from garden soil or compost? Try making some predictions and then designing experiments to test what you have predicted.

Another possible project is to compare your oil-eating microbes with commercially available organisms. Pure cultures of fungi such as *Penicillium* and bacteria such as *Pseudomonas* are sold by biological supply companies as examples of microbes that can be used to clean up oil spills. How do your homegrown colonies compare with commercial cultures in terms of their ability to digest motor oil? Do you think that the microbes that perform best under laboratory conditions will also be effective oil-eaters on beaches and rocky shorelines? What considerations would need to be taken into account in making this prediction?

FORMS FOR INTERACTIVE RESEARCH

See Table 4 (p. 12) in the *Teacher Edition* for a description of where each of these forms fits in the Environmental Inquiry research process.

PLANNING RESEARCH

CHOOSING A RESEARCH TOPIC

Name _____ Date _____

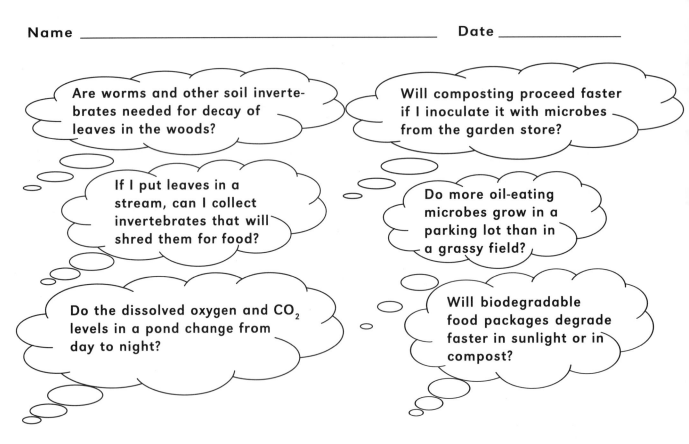

1. Make a list here of questions that you would be interested in investigating using *Decay and Renewal* protocols.

    Example: Does moisture level affect the rate of biodegradation in compost?

2. **Of these questions, which seem the most important and interesting? Pick three:**

   1.

   2.

   3.

3. **For each of the three questions you have chosen, think of how you might design an experiment. Then fill out Table 3.2.**

TABLE 3.2
Potential Research Questions

Question	Brief description of research you might do to address this question	What equipment and supplies would you need?	How long would it take to carry out this project?	Would fieldwork or travel to field sites be required?
Example: Does moisture level affect the rate of biodegradation in compost?	*Build three bioreactors and fill them with the same ingredients except for the amount of water.*	*Soda bottles and other bioreactor supplies, grass clippings, and wood shavings.*	*One period to build the bioreactors, two weeks for composting, then one period to analyze results and clean up.*	*No, we can bring in grass clippings from home and get other supplies at school.*
Question 1:				
Question 2:				
Question 3:				

4. Looking over Table 3.2, consider whether each project would be feasible for you to carry out. Are the equipment and supplies available? Do you have enough time? Will you be able to do whatever fieldwork is needed? Eliminate any questions that do not seem feasible based on logistics such as these.

	Would this project be feasible?	Why or why not?
Example Project	<u>Yes</u> No	*Uses supplies we have available and grass clippings we will bring in from home.*
Project 1	Yes No	
Project 2	Yes No	
Project 3	Yes No	

5. Choose a project you have decided is feasible and interesting, then continue on to **Interactive Research Planning Form #1** or **#2.**

INTERACTIVE RESEARCH PLANNING FORM #1

(for exploratory-level experiments)

Name _____ Date _____

1. **What question have you chosen to investigate, and why?**

   Example: "Are worms and other soil invertebrates needed to break down leaves in the woods?" This question is important because it will help us to figure out whether microbes can break down leaves alone, or whether they need invertebrates to shred the leaves first.

2. **Briefly describe a project you would like to do to address this question.**

   Example: We plan to make containers out of nylon stockings, which will keep most invertebrates out but allow water and air to pass through. We'll fill them with leaves and put them in the woods by the school.

3. **What supplies will you need? How will you get any that are not already available in our classroom?**

   Example: We'll need the materials listed in Protocol 2, including a microscope, to check for tiny organisms that might fit through the stocking mesh. We'll also need a scale for observing and weighing the leaves. We'll bring nylon stockings from home and collect leaves from the woods.

INTERACTIVE RESEARCH PLANNING FORM #1
(continued)

4. **How do you plan to schedule your project?**

   Example: We'll need one class period to set up the bags and put them in the woods. Then we'll need one period per month to empty a couple bags, weigh the contents, and collect and observe the organisms and whatever remains of the leaves.

5. **Can you find reports by other students or professional scientists on this topic? If so, what can you learn from what has already been done?**

6. **Meet with another student or group to discuss these plans using the Experimental Design Peer Review Form** (p. 124). **Then describe any changes you've decided to make based on this discussion.**

INTERACTIVE RESEARCH PLANNING FORM #2
(for rigorously designed experiments)

Name _____ Date

1. **What question do you plan to investigate?**

   Example: "Does moisture level affect the rate of biodegradation in compost?"

2. **Why is this question important or relevant to environmental issues?**

   Example: It will help us to figure out whether it is a good idea to add water to compost piles during dry seasons.

3. **Can you find reports by other students or professional scientists on this topic? If so, what can you learn from what has already been done?**

4. **What is your hypothesis (the prediction of what you think will happen, stated in a way that can be tested by doing an experiment)? Why did you choose this prediction?**

   Example: The composting will work best with a moderate amount of added water. We're making this prediction because Chapter 2 says that compost microbes need water for growth, but with too much water the airflow may get blocked.

INTERACTIVE RESEARCH PLANNING FORM #2
(continued)

5. What is your **independent variable** (the factor that you will change to make one treatment different from another)?

    Example: Our independent variable will be the amount of water in the compost mixture.

6. What is your **dependent variable**? (This is the factor you will measure to determine the results of the experiment—it is called "dependent" because the results depend on changes in the independent variable from one treatment to the next.)

    Example: Our dependent variable will be the temperature of the compost. We will measure temperature every day and compare how high it rises and how long it remains hot in the three types of compost.

> If you are confused about the independent and dependent variables, it may help to think back to your research question and then think about how you might want to present the results of your experiment.
>
> On the x-axis is your independent variable. These are the numbers that you decide in advance, to create your various treatments.
>
> On the y-axis is your dependent variable. This is the factor you will be measuring in your experiment.

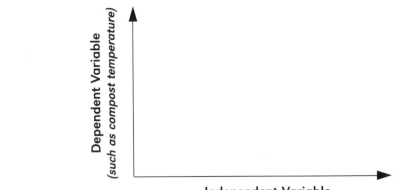

INTERACTIVE RESEARCH PLANNING FORM #2
(continued)

7. What **treatments** do you plan? (Each level of your independent variable is a treatment. You should plan to change only the independent variable from one treatment to the next, keeping all other conditions constant.)

Example: We plan to build six bioreactors and fill them with grass clippings and wood shavings. We will add no water to two bioreactors, as much water as the grass and wood shavings will soak up in two more, and half this amount in the final two.

8. How many **replicates** will you have for each treatment? (The more replicates you can manage, the better, but you will have to figure out how many are feasible for your experiment.)

Example: We will have two replicates of each treatment. These will be the two bioreactors that have the same moisture content.

9. What is your **control** (the untreated group that serves as a standard of comparison)?

Example: The control will be the two bioreactors with no water added. Everything else will be kept the same as in the bioreactors with added water.

10. What factors will you keep **constant** for all treatments? (The constants in an experiment are all the factors that do not change.)

Example: All the bioreactors will be identical and will be filled with the same ingredients except for the amount of water. We will store them under the same conditions at room temperature out of direct sunlight.

INTERACTIVE RESEARCH PLANNING FORM #2
(continued)

11. **What equipment and supplies will you need?**

Example: We'll need all the materials listed in Protocol 12, but just one thermometer because we can use it in all the bioreactors. We'll bring in grass clippings and soda bottles from home.

12. **What schedule will you follow?**

Example: One class period to set up and fill the bioreactors, then for two weeks we'll just need a few minutes each day to take temperature readings. After two weeks we'll need another class period to take them apart and analyze the contents.

13. **What will you measure, and how will you display your data? Sketch an empty data table here, with the appropriate headings. (Think about what kind of table you will need to record the data from your experiment.)**

On this graph, add labels for the x-axis and y-axis and sketch your expected results.

INTERACTIVE RESEARCH PLANNING FORM #2
(continued)

A Final Check: Evaluate Your Experimental Design

1. Does your planned experiment actually test your *hypothesis*?

2. Are you changing only one *variable* at a time? Which one?

3. Will your *control* be exposed to exactly the same conditions as your treatments (except for the *independent variable*)?

4. How many *replicates* will you have for each *treatment*?

5. Meet with another student or group to discuss these plans using the **Experimental Design Peer Review Form** (p. 124). Then describe any changes you've decided to make based on this discussion.

PRESENTING RESEARCH RESULTS

RESEARCH REPORT FORM

Name _____ Date _____

1. What is the title of your research project?

2. What is your research question? Why is this question important, or how is it relevant to environmental issues?

3. Have other people investigated this question, or a similar one? Summarize what you have learned about this question from other students' reports, or from library or Internet research.

4. Summarize your procedures here.

RESEARCH REPORT FORM *(continued)*

5. Make a table here to summarize your data. Include calculations such as the averages of all replicates for each treatment.

6. Graph your data. (Remember: The independent variable goes on the x-axis and the dependent variable on the y-axis.)

7. What conclusions can you reach? (What did you learn from your experiment? Can you think of any other possible explanations for your results?)

8. If you looked into the research by other people on this subject, how do your results agree or disagree with what they found, and why do you think this may be the case?

RESEARCH REPORT FORM *(continued)*

9. What might you change to improve your experimental design?

10. If you had a chance to do another experiment, what would you change in order to learn more about the topic you studied? (Did you come up with questions you can't answer using your data? If so, that's a good starting point for planning future research. What new experiments might help to answer your new questions?)

POSTER GUIDELINES

Posters are one way in which scientists present their research results. When posters are displayed at conferences, researchers have the opportunity to discuss their findings and ideas with fellow scientists.

At a poster session, people tend to spend the most time looking at posters that are attractive, well-organized, and easy to read. It's best to keep the text short and to illustrate your points with graphs, photos, and diagrams.

To make your poster effective, make sure that it is:

Readable—Can your text be read from 2 meters away? (20 points is a good font size)

Understandable—Do your ideas fit together and make sense?

Organized—Is your work summarized clearly and concisely, using the headings listed in the example below?

Attractive—Will your poster make viewers want to take the time to read it? Have you used illustrations and color to enhance your display, without making the text hard to read?

Here is an example poster layout:

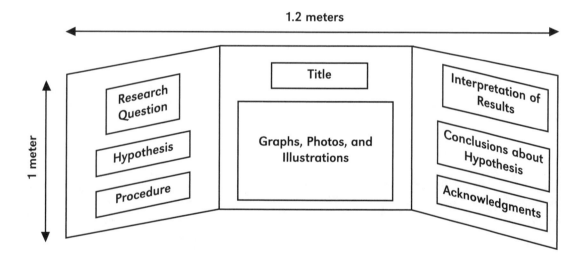

PEER REVIEW

EXPERIMENTAL DESIGN PEER REVIEW FORM

Name of Reviewer _____ **Date** _____

Project Reviewed _____

Is the research question clearly defined?

Very clear	❏	Comments about what was done well:
Mostly clear	❏	
Somewhat clear	❏	Suggestions for improvement:
Largely unclear	❏	

Are the procedures clearly described?

Very clear	❏	Comments about what was done well:
Mostly clear	❏	
Somewhat clear	❏	Suggestions for improvement:
Largely unclear	❏	

How well do the procedures address the research question?

Very well	❏	Comments about what was done well:
OK	❏	
Minor problems	❏	Suggestions for improvement:
Needs work	❏	

RESEARCH REPORT PEER REVIEW FORM

Name of Reviewer _____ Date _____

Project Reviewed _____

After reading a research report written by other students, answer the following questions. Remember to keep your answers friendly and constructive.

1. What was a particular strength in this experimental design?

2. Do you agree with the conclusions? Do they appear to be supported by the results of the experiment?

3. What suggestions can you make for improving this experiment or report?

POSTER PEER REVIEW FORM

Name of Reviewer _____   Date _____

Project Reviewed   _____

KEY
1—Largely unclear
2—Somewhat clear
3—Mostly clear
4—Very clear

	(−) (+)
Does the poster include: Title, Research Question, Hypothesis, Procedure, Results, Conclusions, and Acknowledgments?	1 2 3 4
Is there a clear statement of the research question and hypothesis?	1 2 3 4
Does the experiment appear to be designed appropriately to address the research question?	1 2 3 4
Are the procedures described in enough detail for the experiment to be copied by someone else?	1 2 3 4
Are the data presented clearly?	1 2 3 4
Is there a clear explanation of the results?	1 2 3 4
Do the conclusions seem well supported by the data?	1 2 3 4
Were the presenters able to answer questions clearly?	1 2 3 4
Is the poster attractive and easy to read and understand?	1 2 3 4

TOTAL SCORE   _____

Comments:
What was a particular strength of this experimental design?

What suggestions do you have for improving either this experiment or the poster presentation?

INTERACTIVE RESEARCH:
WASTEWATER TREATMENT DESIGN CHALLENGE

WASTEWATER TREATMENT DESIGN CHALLENGE

When engineers and scientists design systems for wastewater treatment, they must meet certain criteria concerning treatment effectiveness, and they also have to work within specified constraints such as cost. Balancing needs and constraints demands critical thinking, creativity, and skills in mathematical analysis, scientific inquiry, and technological design. In the scenario described below, you will be given a design challenge that will make use of your knowledge and skills related to biodegradation.

Materials

▶ Selected construction materials (see **Parts List and Cost Analysis Form**, p. 136)

▶ Water quality test kits or probes for turbidity, dissolved oxygen, and nutrients such as phosphate, nitrate, and ammonia-nitrogen

▶ Lab notebook

▶ **Parts List and Cost Analysis Form** (p. 136)

▶ **Design Selection Rubric** (p. 137)

▶ **Design Proposal Form** (p. 138)

▶ **Design Challenge Peer Review Form** (p. 140)

Setting the Scene

The town of Forest Hills has a problem. Many residents are moving into town, and many new homes and businesses are being built to accommodate this population growth. Until now, each home or business has had a septic system for wastewater disposal. (A septic system is an underground tank in which solids settle, followed by a series of perforated pipes from which the remaining wastewater filters through the soil). Septic systems will no longer be an acceptable option in Forest Hills because the town's well water would become contaminated by too much wastewater leaching downward into the groundwater.

Although everyone wants their water supply to be clean and safe, the residents of Forest Hills do not want their taxes to go up to pay for adequate wastewater treatment. You work for a consulting firm hired by the town to figure out a way to adequately treat the wastewater at minimal cost. You will be carrying out laboratory-scale tests to determine the most efficient and cost-effective way to treat the town's wastewater.

Forest Hills's wastewater will include water from toilets, showers, sinks, washing machines, and dishwashers. In fact, it will include all the water that goes down the drains in the town's homes, schools, businesses, and industries. However, it will not include storm-water runoff because the town has already decided to install storm sewers that will send runoff directly into a nearby stream rather than to the treatment plant. The town planners have chosen a site for the new wastewater treatment plant and have decided that the treated effluent will discharge into Mirror Lake. This lake is popular for swimming and boating but has begun to have nuisance blooms of algae during the summer months. Town officials have asked your firm to make sure that the treated wastewater will not increase these eutrophication problems.

The Challenge

Build and test a model of a wastewater treatment system that adequately removes unwanted solids, dissolved organic matter, and nutrients. You will not need to treat the solids that you remove from solution. Although wastewater treatment normally includes a step to kill germs, you will not need to include disinfection in your treatment design because the synthetic wastewater you will be using will not contain disease-causing organisms.

The SciLink sites found using the code below provide information about wastewater treatment processes, including use of alum for phosphorus removal and activated carbon for removal of odors, colors, and some types of contaminants.

SCI
LINKS.
THE WORLD'S A CLICK AWAY

Topic: wastewater treatment
Go to: www.sciLINKS.org
Code: DR12

Design Criteria and Constraints

Treatment

▶ The system must be able to treat one liter of synthetic wastewater, which will be provided.

▶ The treatment should lower the turbidity, biological oxygen demand, and nutrient content of the wastewater, measured using tests specified by your teacher.

▶ The treatment should not add new contaminants to the water.

Schedule

▶ Final water quality tests will be run one week after system start-up, so treatment must be completed within one week.

Cost

▶ The cost of the system should be as low as possible to provide effective treatment.

Safety

▶ The system must pose no hazards to users or observers.

Maintenance

▶ As part of your report, you will need to describe and provide a cost estimate for any routine maintenance needed before the system can be reused with a new batch of wastewater.

Durability

▶ The system should be capable of performing several tests without major repairs.

▶ It should be easy to transport your system and rebuild it at a new site.

Restrictions

▶ Your model is limited to a maximum of five separate containers for filtration and/or storage.

▶ Your model must fit within an area of 1 m^2.

The Design Process

Step 1. Define the Problem

1. Along with the members of your team, read Setting the Scene, The Challenge, and Design Criteria and Constraints. These will give you an overview of the problem and the specifications you will be working with.

2. Read Chapters 1 and 2 for background information on wastewater treatment and related biodegradation processes in nature. For additional information, check the SciLinks (p. 130) for specifics about wastewater treatment techniques.

3. Think about what types of pollutants are likely to be in Forest Hills's wastewater. Record all appropriate information in your lab notebook.

4. Discuss with your teacher what parameters you will measure at the end of the process to assess the effectiveness of your treatment system. (These parameters will vary depending on what types of water quality testing equipment are available.)

5. Write a statement of the problem that you will be attempting to solve and any ideas you have come up with about design possibilities. Think about how physical, biological, and chemical processes are used in wastewater treatment plants and how you might use one or more of these processes in your own treatment design.

Step 2. Identify Design Solutions and Select the Best Alternative

1. Examine the parts listed in the **Parts List and Cost Analysis Form**. This list includes materials that can be used to build a wide variety of devices. Brainstorm possible ways of using appropriate materials to construct a treatment system that meets your specific criteria. Make a list in your lab notebook of all possibilities developed by members of your team. Include a sketch for each alternative developed.

2. Calculate the cost of each of your designs and record in your lab notebook.

3. If necessary, brainstorm ideas for reducing costs of one or more of the designs. Recalculate the costs and record all changes in your notebook.

4. In order to select the best alternative, your team will need to determine the advantages and disadvantages of each of the proposed designs. The **Design Selection Rubric** provides a systematic way of ranking your choices, but feel free to customize it or to build your own. A design rubric should include a list of the specifications that you want to use in judging each alternative, and a rating scale. For example, you could use a scale of 1 to 3: (1 = poor, 2 = acceptable, 3 = good).

Example Use of a Design Selection Rubric

Design Alternative	Expected Treatment Effectiveness	Cost	Safety	Expected Maintenance Cost	Expected Durability	Total
Idea #1	2	2	3	2	2	11
Idea #2	1	2	3	2	2	10
Idea #3	3	1	3	2	3	12*
Idea #4	2	1	3	1	2	9

*In this example, Idea #3 appears to be the best because it scored the highest for this combination of specifications.

5. As a team, discuss the trade-offs you had to make in selecting the best alternative. It's possible that you won't be satisfied with the design you've chosen because this process doesn't account for the fact that some specifications may be more important than others. To take this into account, you could make a more complicated rubric in which you multiply scores by weighting factors that you have assigned to each column.

6. Once you have selected your best alternative, use the **Design Proposal Form** to sketch and describe your ideas for review by your teacher.

Step 3. Build, Test, and Use the Best Design

1. Construct your wastewater treatment system using the materials from the parts list and any other acceptable materials that you have included in your design. As you work on construction, you may need to refine, eliminate, or add new parts to your design. Record all modifications in your notebook.

2. Test your device using tap water. It may be a good idea to test individual parts of your system before you test it as a whole. Use the **Design Challenge Peer Review Form** to see how your system will be evaluated when you give your final presentation, and make any modifications you think will help to improve it. Repeat the testing and modification until you are satisfied with your system, recording all the steps as you go along.

3. Set up the system to run for one week of treatment.

Step 4. Evaluate the Constructed System

1. Using the effluent from your treatment system, run water quality tests specified by your teacher to determine how well the treatment has worked.

2. Record the results of your assessment in your lab notebook and fill in the **Design Challenge Peer Review Form** as a self-assessment of your system.

Step 5. Plan Your Presentation

1. In your team, plan a presentation to illustrate how the system you built meets the specifications and constraints that were provided. Be specific about the features and advantages of your device. All the teams have tried to minimize costs and meet treatment specifications, so rather than claim that you have minimized costs, report precisely how much you have spent. Include a demonstration of the operation of your sampler.

2. Take another look at the **Design Challenge Peer Review Form**. Other students will use this to evaluate your presentation, and you can use it yourself as a checklist of topics you will need to address.

3. Once your team is clear about the important details to be conveyed, determine what presentation aids you will use. You may want to prepare a handout for the class or create transparencies to show on an overhead projector. If time permits, you might decide to use a computer presentation.

4. Decide who will present each topic, and set time limits based on how much time you will have for the entire presentation.

Step 6. Present Your Work

1. Give your presentation and ask for questions.

2. Pass out the **Design Challenge Peer Review Form** to get feedback from your classmates.

FORMS FOR WASTEWATER TREATMENT DESIGN CHALLENGE

WASTEWATER TREATMENT DESIGN CHALLENGE
Parts List and Cost Analysis Form

Item	Cost per Item ($)	Quantity Needed	Cost Subtotal
Plastic soda bottle (any size)	0.05		
Tubing	1.50/m		
Straight connector for tubing	1.80		
T connector for tubing	1.00		
Duct tape	0.15/m		
Stopper	0.15		
Screen—10 cm^2	0.75		
Gravel—100 g	0.50		
Sand—100 g	0.75		
Aerator	3.00		
Bucket	2.00		
Activated charcoal—10 g	1.00		
Alum—10 g	0.75		
Source of microbes*—10 g	0.25		
Coffee filter	0.10		
Duckweed or other aquatic plants (free if collected by students)	1.00		
Other:			
TOTAL COST			$

*In activated sludge treatment systems, sewage sludge is added back into the system as a rich source of microbes capable of digesting organic matter. Sludge is not an option for classroom projects because it contains disease-causing organisms, but a wide range of microbes can be found in samples of compost, soil, or sediment from a pond or stream.

Cost Analysis Instructions

▶ Under **Quantity Needed**, enter the number of pieces or estimated length of each item you plan to use.

▶ Multiply the numbers in column 2 by column 3 to obtain the subtotal for each item.

▶ Sum the subtotals in column 4 to determine the total cost of your design.

Other Materials: If approved by your teacher, you may use materials other than those listed above, with prices based on those listed in commercial catalogs.

WASTEWATER TREATMENT DESIGN CHALLENGE
Design Selection Rubric

Use this form to help in selecting your best design idea. If you decide to carry out extensive revisions after pilot testing your design, you might want to fill out this form again to select the best modification of your original design.

Design Alternative	Expected Treatment Effectiveness	Cost	Safety	Expected Maintenance Cost	Expected Durability	Other Factors	TOTAL
Idea #1							
Idea #2							
Idea #3							
Idea #4							

SCALE
1 = poor
2 = acceptable
3 = good

WASTEWATER TREATMENT DESIGN CHALLENGE
Design Proposal Form

Name _____ Date _____

Sketch your proposed design for a wastewater treatment system that meets the specified criteria and constraints:

Will you need any supplies that are not on the approved list? If so, what will you need, and how do you plan to get them?

What will your system cost?

What kinds of treatment will your system use?

Physical treatment:

__ screening or filtration

__ settling

__ aeration

__ other (describe)

Chemical treatment:

What chemical do you plan to use?

What do you hope to accomplish with this chemical?

Biological treatment:

What type of organisms do you plan to use?

What role will these organisms play in treating the wastewater?

If you plan to use microorganisms, what will be the source?

DESIGN CHALLENGE PEER REVIEW FORM

Presenters:_____

Assessed by: _____

Date: _____

Criteria	Evaluation (-) (+)	Weight	Points
The system is safe to handle and operate.	1 2 3 4 5	1 3 5	
The cost of the system is low.	1 2 3 4 5	1 3 5	
The system fits within 1 m^2 area.	1 2 3 4 5	1 3 5	
The system is capable of performing several tests without repair.	1 2 3 4 5	1 3 5	
The design was based on appropriate principles of wastewater treatment.	1 2 3 4 5	1 3 5	
New contaminants did not appear to be added to the water during treatment.	1 2 3 4 5	1 3 5	
Treatment reduced the turbidity of the water.	1 2 3 4 5	1 3 5	
Nitrate and/or ammonia-N concentrations were reduced.	1 2 3 4 5	1 3 5	
Phosphate concentrations were reduced.	1 2 3 4 5	1 3 5	
Biological oxygen demand was reduced.	1 2 3 4 5	1 3 5	
Reasonable explanations were provided of the treatment system and its results.	1 2 3 4 5	1 3 5	
The presenters provided clear answers to any questions that were raised.	1 2 3 4 5	1 3 5	
		Total Points:	

In each row, multiply the **Evaluation** score by the **Weight** (assigned by the teacher) to get the **Point** score. Then sum the numbers in column 4 to get the **Total Points**.

Comments:

What was a particular strength of this wastewater treatment design?

What suggestions do you have for improving either this design or the way in which it was presented?